NO NEED FOR SPEED

A beginner's guide to the joy of running

JOHN BINGHAM COLUMNIST FOR **RUNNER'S** WORLD

RODALE

LIVE YOUR WHOLE LIFE™

This edition first published in the UK in 2004 by
Rodale International Ltd
7–10 Chandos Street
London W1G 9AD
www.rodale.co.uk

Runner's World is a registered trademark of Rodale Inc.

Printed and bound in the UK by CPI Bath using acid-free paper from sustainable sources.

1 3 5 7 9 8 6 4 2

Cover and Interior Designer: Christopher Rhoads
Cover Photographer: Mitch Mandel

A CIP record of this book is available from the British Library
ISBN 1-4050-6724-1

This paperback edition distributed to the book trade by Pan Macmillan Ltd

Visit us on the Web at *www.runnersworld.co.uk*

Notice
This book is intended to help you make decisions regarding your fitness and exercise programme. It is not intended as a substitute for professional fitness and medical advice. As with all exercise programmes, you should seek your doctor's approval before you begin.

Contents

Part 1: Inspiration

Part 2: Perspiration

Acknowledgements

Writing the acknowledgements for my first book was probably a lot like planning an acceptance speech for an Academy Award. I wanted to thank everyone I'd ever known because I wasn't sure I'd ever get another chance. Now, for my second book, I have another chance.

It's surprising that most of the people I thanked last time are the same people I need to thank this time. Those who have supported me most unconditionally, the friends and family who stayed through my metamorphosis, are still here. For that, and to them, I am eternally grateful.

But there are a few new faces, most notably three young editors – Susan Lindfors, Mark Remy and Jane Hahn – who have continued to make me sound smarter than I'll ever be. In their own way, each has helped make me a better writer and, more important, a better person.

And Alisa Bauman, a wonderful young editor, who served as the chief editor of this project. Alisa demonstrated a remarkable talent for breathing life into my writing and polishing my thoughts until they are brilliant. She has taken my vision of what this book could be and made it a reality. I am astonished at her patience and skill.

Jenny Hadfield, a great friend and uncompromising coach, has taught me that wanting to be a better runner isn't enough. You have to know *how* to get better. With her gentle but unrelenting guidance, I am stronger, healthier and better able to take on the challenges of running and living than at any time in my life. This book could not have been written without her help.

In the past three years, I've seen thousands of new faces at the starting lines of large and small road races around the country. They are the faces of those who have discovered, as I did, that running isn't only about miles and pace. It's about people. It's about finding the best in ourselves and the best in each other. These new runners are the heart and soul of the sport. They are a never-ending source of inspiration for me. I'm grateful that they have chosen to join me on this journey.

As with my last book, I must again thank two important people for their influence and impact on this book and my life. They are Amby Burfoot and my wife, Karen. Amby gave me the opportunity to have the life that I have. He took the risk of giving me – an old, slow runner and an unknown with no background or training as a writer – a column in the world's premier running magazine. Every day I try to affirm his faith in me.

And Karen … whose meaning in my life transcends any label like wife or partner or friend. She has been, and continues to be, an inseparable part of my spirit. She is the one who has held the ladder as I've climbed to my destiny.

Introduction

People will tell you lots of good reasons to start running: lose weight, get fit, have a healthier heart, relieve stress and lower your cholesterol, to name a few. In my experience, those happen to be just about the *worst* reasons to run.

I've heard runners talking to non-runners. Runners almost always start by telling the would-be runner about all the legitimate-sounding reasons to run. For some reason, runners are afraid to tell people the *real* reason they run. We like it! We really like it.

The truth is that very few people are willing to get up at 5.00 am, pull on running shoes and step out into the rain just to lower their cholesterol levels a few points. No, it isn't that way. We runners run in the rain and cold and in the heat and humidity because *not* running is unthinkable.

I spent most of my life thinking that runners were lunatics. I saw them on the back roads where I lived in the middle of the winter and thought they were totally mad. Now when I'm out running on a lakefront path in sub-zero temperatures, I *know* that they are totally mad. I also know that I've become just as crazy as they are. And just as content.

Running doesn't have to be a 'full speed ahead' kind of affair. It *can* be. You'll find many books that will tell you how to run your fastest 5-K or how to lower your marathon time by an hour. This is not one of those books. This is a book about how you can discover the joy that comes from moving your body with your own two feet.

The words used in this book are different. When I talk about running, I'm really talking about running and walking. I don't distinguish between the two. When I run, I also walk. When I walk, I also run. I mix the two activities together in order to be able to enjoy and participate in the kinds of events I want to do.

With this book, anyone can be a runner. You need only to have a willingness to forget everything you thought you knew about running and almost everything you thought you knew about yourself. Running isn't what it was in the 1970s. Chances are that you aren't either.

No Need for Speed will help you develop a strategy for success. Throughout the plan, you'll discover the 'whys' and the 'hows' of running, what you'll need, what you'll want, what you'll do right, and what you'll do wrong. In the process, you'll gain many insights into the you that you're dreaming of becoming.

Many books about running take a linear approach. This method works well if all you intend to do is run your fastest 5-K or marathon and then give up. *No Need for Speed* is based on a more realistic 'circle of success'. You'll travel through the cycle of inspiration, perspiration, dedication and celebration that I introduced in *The Courage to Start: A Guide to Running for Your Life* (Simon & Schuster, 1999). You'll learn how to keep finding the inspiration that leads to perspiration, dedication, and celebration through running. Here's how each stage in that cycle works:

1. Inspiration: for the first few weeks of a fitness programme, inspiration often comes naturally. The five chapters in this section will show you how to keep your inspiration strong long after the initial newness of running has worn off.

2. Perspiration: often, runners fall at one of two extremes. They either push themselves too hard and end up injured or burned out, or they don't push themselves enough. The five chapters in this section will show you how to push yourself just right.

3. Dedication: very different from willpower, dedication comes when running is inherently a part of your life. The five chapters in this section will help you make the switch

from forcing yourself to run, to running simply because you enjoy it.

4. Celebration: finally, it's time to party. When you've reached this stage, you can celebrate all of your hard work with the realization that you are a runner – and you are a winner.

Each of the four sections of No Need for Speed concludes with a 'Basic Truths' chapter. These chapters will help you with the basics of running: how far to run, how to buy shoes, what to wear, how to avoid injuries, how to complement running with other fitness pursuits, and more. These guides will give you the practical information and guidance you need to achieve your running goals. The first basics guide will help you get started, the second will give you information on injury prevention and treatment, the third shows you how to use cross-training to enhance your running, and the fourth is for those of you who believe, as I do, that it is in the fire of racing that we galvanize ourselves as runners.

In every chapter of No Need for Speed, you'll find inspirational advice from people like you who have used running not only as an activity, but also as a medium for exploring themselves and their potential. In each 'Lessons Learned', you'll hear from former beginners who agreed to share their insights. You'll read about ordinary people who have achieved extraordinary things by giving in to the joy of being active.

As you read, you'll also discover that runners are by nature a funny, quirky, disciplined, lazy, opinionated, quiet, helpful, rude, happy and depressed group – just like the rest of the population! Whatever your reasons for running, whatever your reasons for not running, No Need for Speed will help you find your way to becoming yourself.

Waddle on, friends.

Part 1
Inspiration

Seeing the Light

The first step towards lifelong running is simple: forget everything you know about the topic

Three weeks. That's as long as my inspiration lasted. Three weeks. It didn't matter what I decided to do or be, I couldn't get past the first three weeks of any new quest. I got fired up about my newest sport, designed an elaborate plan to propel me to some higher level of fitness, bought all the equipment and clothes, and started with all the enthusiasm I could muster. Knowing how often I'd failed to stick with previous plans didn't prevent me from believing that it would be different this time.

What a three weeks I always had! Nothing quite matches the first blush of enthusiasm for something new. It's like first love – exciting, exhilarating and tempting. The rush that accompanies the first three weeks was enough to keep me coming back for more. The dream of becoming whatever it was I had decided to be was intoxicating.

The beauty of being really bad at something is that you can get better with almost no work. If you don't believe me, borrow a cello. The first week of dragging a bow across the cello's strings will produce sounds usually heard only at catfights. But after annoying everyone within earshot for a week or so, you'll discover that the tune you're playing sounds a little like 'Three Blind Mice'. It may be a scratchy rendition, but with a little imagination, you can actually discern a melody. That's the first mile marker on the road to frustration and doom. You believe that the progress you're experiencing will continue. It won't.

It's easy for mature beginner athletes to imagine that the path to an active life will be linear. The painful moments that accompany your first few attempts at running or walking are quickly replaced by a sense of accomplishment. The idea of moving your body with your own two feet begins to seem like a real possibility. Progress is inevitable in the beginning, but failure looms in the shadows.

My basement is filled with relics of my inspiration. The fishing rod and tackle box from the time I decided to become a professional bass fisherman lay abandoned in a corner for years. For a 3-week period in my life, I actually convinced myself that I could be a *professional* bass fisherman! How hard could it be? All I had to do was be smarter than a *fish*! As it turned out, I wasn't. And my plan sank faster than an anchor.

My home became a museum to failed inspiration. My life was cluttered with the evidence of my inability to stick with any plan. Worse, my soul was cluttered with the remnants of dreams that never came true. I'm not alone. Even when we begin with the best of intentions, it's only a matter of time before our past overtakes most of us.

Inspiration is the match strike. It burns brightly, but only for a short time. Too many exercise programmes and diet gurus rely on this pattern of inspiration and burnout. It can be different. You can learn to go from inspiration to perspiration to dedication to celebration, and then start all over again. And you can do it for the rest of your life. I know because I have, and nothing in my story is that different from yours.

I'm the prototypical mature beginner athlete. My running career, as I like to call it, began around my 43rd birthday. I was a dedicated couch potato. I smoked for 25 years, drank often enough to worry that I might have a problem, and made overeating a way of life. At 1.72 m (5 ft 8 in) and 109 kg (17st 2lb) – 36 kg (5½ st) more than I weigh today – I was well past stout. I was rotund.

Did I care? Not much. You don't get that out of shape overnight. You get there so slowly that you barely realize it's happening. You begin buying clothes a size larger, then another size larger. Before you know it, you're shopping in the 'big and tall' men's shops. You get there by being a little less active each year, until you find that there's very little you can do comfortably. The old manual lawnmower gives way to the riding lawnmower, which gives way to hiring the neighbouring youngster to drive it. Carrying the shopping bags seems a bit harder than before, and you notice that it takes longer and longer to get in and out of the car.

I know because I was there. Pick an excuse for not being active – I've used it. I don't have time or talent. I don't have motivation or discipline. My family doesn't support me. I have small children. I have old children. My job is too stressful.

The truth is that I didn't want to be active. At that time in my life, I was content to watch my body get bigger and bigger. I actually managed to take pride in my increased waist size. After all, I told myself, *fat* is where it's *at*!

lessons learned

I waited a long time to start running because I didn't think I could run fast enough. When I started running at 'only' 4½ miles per hour, a whole new world opened up.

– Allison Proctor, aged 37 Running for 18 months

A Lasting Impression

Why or how does a 43-year-old man who is 36 kg overweight suddenly decide to become an athlete? How does that person wake up and decide that he'll become more active?

This is how it happened. A friend and colleague was diagnosed with adult-onset diabetes. I visited her in the hospital, where I listened as her doctor told her about the changes that she would have to make to her lifestyle. She would have to change the way she ate and the way she thought about food. She would have to be more active. In a moment of weakness, I told her that if *she* would do it, I would, too.

I enjoyed riding my bicycle as a child, so that's where I started. I bought an old 10-speed bike. I had no idea how to work the gears or what to do once I got on the street. So I did what I had done as a child: I rode as much as I could, as far as I could go, as often as I wanted. My legs weren't very happy about it at first. There was very little muscle memory left from my pre-pubescent days as a biker, but there was some spiritual memory. The freedom and sense of escape I'd felt as a child was rekindled.

What I did in those early months wasn't 'training'. It was more about trying not to get hurt than trying to get better. I managed to add miles a little at a time, worked out how to get my feet in and out of toeclips without falling off the bike, and even to change gears while in motion.

In another weak moment, I accepted my friend's challenge to ride in a metric century (62 miles) bike event. On a bitterly cold morning I found myself pedalling towards a city 31 miles away so that I could turn around and ride back. At the time, it seemed extraordinarily crazy even to me. We probably could have finished sooner if we hadn't stopped every hour for a smoke. Yes, a smoke! I was willing to be more active and to be careful about what and how much I ate. I was even willing to drink a little less. But giving up smoking was unthinkable. Not yet.

We finished 8½ hours after we started. Sitting in a local restaurant reflecting on what we had accomplished, I felt the first pangs of pride. I had done it. I had actually prepared for and completed a 62-mile bike ride. The feelings were strange. Feeling good about myself was strange to me at first, but I knew I wanted the feelings to continue.

Soon after that ride, I bought my first pair of running shoes. I was on the threshold of becoming a runner.

It may not happen this way for you, but I knew immediately that running was what I wanted to do. (I say running, but from my first attempt, running for me was a matter of running *and* walking, of doing whatever I needed to do to keep moving forwards.) Running was pure. Running was simple. Running was as elemental as it could possibly be. I was all alone when I ran. There were no machines, gears, choices, decisions and no excuses. I could go only as fast as I could go. I could go only as far as my feet would carry me.

Your First Step

Anyone can be more active. Anyone can take the time to gently convince his body that moving is better than not moving. Anyone who is patient can find a way to live a more dynamic and satisfying life. Whether you're 20 or 70 years old, your future is in your hands. More precisely, your future is in your *feet*.

The first step, if you'll pardon the pun, is to forget everything you have ever believed about running. Everything you think running is and everything you think runners are is almost certainly wrong. If it's not wrong, it's probably no longer accurate.

I've watched more than 100,000 people finish marathons. I've seen every imaginable kind of person cross the line – young people, old people, skinny people, *not* skinny people, male and female, every religious and ethnic group. The love of running unites these people.

During the first running boom in the 1970s, runners were set apart from the rest of us. They seemed to be a different species – to endure more pain, to push to higher limits, and to suffer with greater dignity than the rest of us. In some ways, that's still true.

What's different now is that you can be one of them. You can find out that it's possible for you to push your limits to new highs and lows. You can realize that what always seemed like suffering is really your soul being galvanized in the heat of effort. You can discover that you have a deeper strength than you ever imagined. Nothing stops you except your own inertia. Nothing prevents you from joining the ranks of those who have found the magic in movement. Nothing keeps you from starting or improving except your belief that you can't.

lessons learned

I wish that someone had told me that no matter how far I ran or how long it took me, I was a 'real' runner just by being out there.

**– Anne Koeller, aged 38
Running for 6 years**

an exercise in joy

Even if you haven't actually run, even if you're overweight, even if you were always picked last in gym class, even if you're clumsy, even if you don't own a single piece of fitness equipment, you *are* a runner. You don't have to run fast to be a runner. You don't have to be skinny to be a runner. You don't have to run marathons to be a runner. You only have to want to run.

Take your first step along your path to joyful running right now by writing down all the reasons you can't run, can't be fit and can't possibly become an athlete. Then crumple up that list with all the force you can muster and toss it in the bin. Not the rubbish bin in your kitchen, where you can get it back out and try on those 'can'ts' again for size, but the nearest roadside waste disposal unit. Bin those can'ts. You can run. You are a runner.

For 43 years, I was trapped in my own false beliefs. I was trapped in a history of clumsiness and dropped catches. Like so many other less-than-athletically-gifted children, I learned quickly that I was different. All of that can change with a single step. All the memories of failure and disappointment can be wiped out. Everything you've dreamed you can be, all the moments you've wished you could have, are out there for you. The secret is that there is no secret. The magic is that there is no magic. The answers you are looking for lie somewhere between the bottom of your shoes and the road beneath your feet.

Tied in Nots

Real and lasting inspiration comes by overcoming your doubts and fears, one step at a time. With each step forwards, it becomes more difficult not to be an athlete

Like many adults, I knew that being more active would be a good thing. Unless you've been living on another planet for the past 50 years, you know that even small amounts of exercise result in very real benefits.

I knew I would never stick with a programme that required me to go to a gym. I was far too self-conscious about how I looked for that. So running alone on the streets and pavements seemed like the best approach. That way, if I was terrible or if I looked awful, no one else would know.

It never occurred to me to do more than run and walk a little. I didn't dream of running long distances or even of racing. I just wanted to move more, lose some weight, firm up key parts of my body that were jiggling more than they used to, and start to feel better. My fitness goals may have seemed modest to some, but they were monumental to me.

I wasn't willing to go all the way, though. Many of us aren't willing to change our eating habits, drink less or, like me, give up smoking. Our goal is simply to incorporate the amount of activity needed to overcome the rest of our lifestyles. You may think that this approach is unusual, but it's not. I remember coming in from my early runs, collapsing on the sofa and lighting up a cigarette. It made my son crazy.

Change Is Scary

It's a mistake to believe that those of us who have changed our bodies and our lives through activity have done so because we had a dramatic, life-altering revelation. I've talked to very few adult athletes who have had such an experience. It's more likely that we are dragged kicking and screaming into our new lives. If you're like me, you'll cling desperately to your old habits.

I was angry that how I lived my life was going to have to change. I was angry that I was 43 years old and 36 kg (5½ st) overweight. I was angry that it was getting more and more difficult to walk up steps, mow the lawn or wash the car. I was angry that I couldn't live an irresponsible lifestyle and still be thin, fit and healthy. I was *angry*!

I didn't understand why the lifestyle that had worked for me for so many years wasn't working anymore. After all, I had abused my body for most of my life. I was the one who was able to push myself when everyone else around me had to stop. I was the one who could live on cigarettes and coffee for days at a time. I was not going to change any more than I had to. I was *not* going to stop doing the things I enjoyed.

You may be feeling the same way. You may remember the years when you could eat whatever you wanted, go without sleep, drink or smoke with abandon, and still 'play' on the weekends. You may remember a time when your body was willing to forgive you for your indiscretions. If it hasn't already happened, eventually you'll be looking back at a time and a body that are gone forever.

When it finally occurred to me that I had no choice but to be more active, I didn't embrace the idea with enthusiasm. I was grumpy. I put

an exercise in joy

When pursuing any dream, we all have fears and doubts. Take a moment to list all of the things that are tying you in 'nots'. What parts of yourself might you lose if you become a runner? Then, next to all of those fears, list everything that you might gain by becoming a runner. Use this list to galvanize your growth towards a new you.

on the shoes and shorts of a runner, but I did so like a man going to his execution. I knew I had to pay the price to get healthy and fit, but I was hoping I could get a discount.

Of course, I liked the idea that I was wogging (my combination of waddling and jogging) several days a week. I liked the idea that I was actually running in legitimate running shoes. In the first few months, though, I liked the thought of being a runner much more than running. I liked the thought that *other* people thought I was a runner much more than I liked running.

I wasn't ready to give in to the idea that my life was going to have to change. I lived in a strange kind of conflict with myself. I fought the idea of change even as I enjoyed the changes. I prepared to return to my previous lifestyle even as I constructed a training plan for months into the future.

This conflict is a subtle way of setting ourselves up for failure. If we keep the path to our former selves clear and open, it will be easier to go back to it when we finally come to our senses. If we allow ourselves to go too far towards our dream, it will become harder and harder not to achieve it.

I wasn't ready to start thinking like an athlete. I wasn't ready to believe that I could be an athlete. I wasn't ready to believe that I was entitled to think and feel and act like an athlete. I was still overweight. I was still slow. How could that person be an athlete? The biggest problem was that I was not ready to act like a runner when I wasn't running. I was not going to become one of *those* people. Not me!

I was going to be the one who found a way to be both decadent *and* fit. I was going to be the one who could overeat and overtrain. I wanted to be the person who discovered the secret of how to change without changing, how to grow without growing, and how to become a whole new me without losing the old me.

For the better part of a year, I managed to be both what I had been and what I was trying to be. I managed to be actively inactive. I managed to lose weight, get fitter, run further, run faster, and still ignore what was happening to my body and my spirit. During that first year, I lived in a kind of no-man's-land between the past and the future.

But in spite of my determination not to change, I did. The process of becoming a runner began with my first running step. It will for you, too. Even though you may not know it, even though you may be unable or unwilling to acknowledge it to yourself, the act of running changes you.

Turning Fear into Courage

Eventually, you'll begin to realize that your priorities are changing. The more miles that are behind you, the more you think about the miles ahead of you. The more you run, the more you are a runner. It sounds simple and it is. There's nothing more to becoming a runner than running. It isn't how fast or how far you run. It isn't even how long you've been running. It's only that you run that makes you a runner.

It becomes more and more difficult *not* to be an athlete – not by design, but by default. You begin to look forward to the feelings ofeffort that you once avoided. Instead of shunning the fatigue of honest effort, you go out of your way to find opportunities to exert yourself. Eventually, I even found myself thinking like an athlete when I wasn't running. The first change I noticed was that I began to look at food differently. The more I learned about how my body used the food I put into it, the more I tried to make choices that would enhance my athletic performance. I was surprised to find that those choices were much easier when I thought like an athlete.

Another curious change was that I began to view other runners differently. I had never expected to be able to relate to the joys and frustrations of other runners. I never expected to be able to talk to them about my running. I didn't expect them to be as understanding of my struggles. Suddenly, I was part of something. I was part of the running community. The more open I was about my running, the more open others were about theirs. I found out that runners love to talk about running. As I began to hear their stories, I became less and less worried about my story.

We all tend to believe that our lives are somehow unique, that our situation is radically different from anyone else's. We believe we've got to the current place in our lives by a path that no one else has travelled. We believe we got overweight and out of shape in some peculiar way. We often use these beliefs as excuses to stay tied in 'nots'. If no one can understand the uniqueness of our situation, then no one can offer

lessons learned

Looking back, I now realize that I did not have to fear that others would laugh at me for being slow or fat or white or brunette or whatever else I worried about before or during runs or races. I have found that most people are either supportive of a beginner's efforts or so scared themselves that they are completely unconcerned with how anyone else runs or looks. The others who are mean enough to say something hurtful, well, the longer I run, the more confident I get, and the less I care about what someone like that thinks.

– Melissa Scott, aged 28
Running for 2 years

advice on how to get out of it. No person, book or plan can possibly address our particular situation. We convince ourselves that we're all alone.

Many Runners, One Road

The revelation that came to me from talking to other runners is that the road to a healthier, more active life is the same for everyone. The process is the same whether you become a world-record holder, an age-group champion or a solidly back-of-the-pack runner like me. You just have to be willing to see where you are, decide where you want to be and work out how you want to get there.

As I looked at other runners differently, I began to look at myself differently. As I heard their success stories and understood that they were like me, I started to believe that maybe I could be something more, and less, than I had been.

Don't misunderstand, I wasn't very happy about it at first. Standing at the starting line of a race in sub-freezing temperatures one Saturday morning, I found myself questioning my own sanity. Surely there was another way. What had happened to the person who drank coffee and smoked cigarettes on cold weekend mornings? Where had he gone? Surely he had enough sense to stay inside.

lessons learned

Running is a whole-being activity; running is life-changing. Running has healed my body of a chronic condition, nourished my spirit and sharpened my mind. It's proven to me that I can do almost anything if I simply give it my best effort and believe. If I had known that this would happen, I would have started running many years before I did.

– Beth Miller, aged 37
Running for 5 years

Putting on a pair of running shoes doesn't make you immune from the doubts that haunt all of us. But running shoes can help you understand that those doubts often fuel the engine of self-discovery. At first, I doubted that I could run a mile. Then I doubted that I could finish a 5-K. It was my doubt that drove me to learn more, to train smarter and to achieve new goals.

As I set new goals, conquered new fears and overcame new doubts, I became a new person. I was no longer the person who sat inside on cold mornings. I was not the person for whom comfort was the sole objective. I wasn't the person who was controlled by the circumstances of my life. I was a runner. I was one of those people who ran in the cold, rain, heat and humidity. I was one of those people who wore shorts and tights in public. I was one of those people who stretched while standing in the queue at the supermarket.

Even now, I'm amused at all the things I am – a marathon runner, a triathlete, an adventurer – and all because I'm willing to move my body with my own two feet. What happens when we untie the 'nots' in our lives is that we can see beyond today and begin to imagine a different tomorrow. As you see the obvious changes in your body, you also begin to see the less obvious changes in your soul.

When you untie the 'nots', when you become fully engaged in the process of becoming a better athlete, you can't help becoming a better person. You find, without realizing it, that you're *not* afraid to change, learn and grow. You learn to look past all the things that you can't be to those few that you can. As you learn to accept your limitations as an athlete, you're less afraid to accept the other limitations in your life. Your unique combination of talent and motivation, discipline and dedication, become the tools with which you build the person you most want to be. And that's *not* bad.

Getting Real

Until you exorcise the memories that keep you from succeeding, there's no point in exercising your body. You can be the best runner you can be, if you're realistic about your abilities and your goals

You may be uncomfortable hearing that no one can tell you what your fitness goals should be. No one can tell you how much activity is right for you, what eating strategy will work best, or how long it will take to achieve your early fitness goals. It's true that there's no shortage of people who will try. Friends, partners and even authors of books are certain that *they* know what's best for you. They don't.

As a 43-year-old smoker with 36 excess kilos and a long history of overeating, I didn't want to face my own reality. I'd become very good at ignoring my body and even better at ignoring my soul. Getting real was about the last thing on my mind.

You have to get real and stay real. You have to start by being honest with yourself, then continue to look honestly at where you are, where you're going and where you want to be. It isn't always easy and it isn't always fun, but the more honest you are with yourself the more likely you will succeed. This is the first stumbling block towards a life of activity. As a friend once told me, most people spend their lives working at jobs they don't like in order to buy things they don't need in order to impress people they don't know. Most of us don't have much experience with getting real.

What does getting real mean to you? What does getting real have to do with losing weight, getting fit, walking, running and feeling better? It has everything to do with it. It's like asking the question, 'How do you get to Manchester?' It all depends on where you start.

Are you a former school athlete? Were you ever in better shape than you are right now? Do you, as I did, have a history of starting on fitness and weight-loss programmes with unbridled enthusiasm only to fail in a matter of a few weeks? Do you, as I did, have a wardrobe filled with 'fat' clothes, 'thin' clothes, and 'clothes that I'll never be able to wear again, but keep just to make myself feel bad'? Are you returning to running after a few years of inactivity? Are you motivated by the event T-shirts? Do you want a marathon medal? Do you want to start running in order to run or because you think running might be a means to some other end?

These are the easy questions to answer. These are the questions

lessons learned

When I started running, I would run for a relatively short distance at a pace that was too fast for what I was ready for. I think I was trying to keep up with the people that I would see running as I drove around town. I quickly became frustrated and also very short of breath. It was after I finally began to slow myself right down that I was able to sustain a 'run' for any distance. At first, this seemed comical, as my wife could walk at about the pace I was running. What it did, though, was let me feel like I was really running. It also gave me a sense of accomplishment that I could run a mile, or two, and eventually more.

– Dale Wiersma, aged 41
Running for 2 years

that you can work out in a few minutes. But these are not the questions that you need to answer in the long run. Getting real means digging deeper. For me, getting real meant looking honestly at my thoughts and beliefs about myself as an athlete. I had to dig back into my memory and find the beginnings of my opinions about my body, my potential and myself. One particular moment in my life stood out.

Undoing the Damage

Like most 12-year-old boys, I wanted to be an athlete, so I tried out for the school basketball team. Being nearly the youngest in my class and short didn't deter me. I'd seen the uniforms, been to the games and heard the crowd cheering for the players by name. I wanted to be on the team.

In those days, basketball practice was mostly about running up and down the court, doing lay-up drills and shooting free throws. I shot free throws using the two-handed, between-the-legs technique since I wasn't strong enough to shoot the ball overhand. After each practice, I stayed until I had made 20 baskets from the free throw line. The coach was impressed with my tenacity, if not my talent.

Then the moment came. We were behind by one point to our cross-city rivals. There were only a few seconds left when the coach called a timeout. 'Bingham,' he yelled. 'Get ready to go in.' This was a major shock since I had never actually played in a game. I took off my warmup jacket and made my way to the coach's side. The next words out of his mouth stunned everyone. 'Let Bingham take the shot. No one will expect it. No one will be guarding him. Toss him the inbound pass, get out of his way and get under the basket.' Then he turned to me and said, 'Just get close enough to shoot a free throw.'

My heart was pounding and my palms were sweating. As I moved onto the floor, I felt every eye in the auditorium on me. The coach

an exercise *in* joy

Take a moment to think about what's holding you back from your athletic potential. How much time will you have to invest in getting fit? An hour a day? Three hours a week? How much support can you expect from your family and friends? Do you think that the important people in your life will rally around you and embrace your new lifestyle? What other support systems are in place for you? Do you have access to the equipment and information you need to get started? Is there some place you can go to ask questions and to get answers that mean something to you?

Are you ready to accept the limits of your abilities? Are you convinced that if you work hard enough you can be the best runner there is? Or are you ready to accept that if you work hard enough you'll still only be the best runner that you can be? The answers to such questions affect the pace at which you accomplish your goals. Be honest with yourself.

was right. Not one opposing player came within 15 metres of me. The inbound pass came to me, I had the ball in my hands, the coach was yelling, the team was yelling, the crowd was yelling. Then it happened.

I moved towards the basket and managed to dribble the ball once or twice, but instead of taking the underhand shot that I had practised, I drew the ball up and shot it overhand. As I pushed the ball off, I could feel the room go into a state of suspended animation. The world stopped. So did the ball. Well, it didn't actually stop. It just dropped harmlessly to the ground and into the hands of an eager opponent who raced past me and scored an easy basket. We lost the game by three points. Adolescent boys aren't the most forgiving people on Earth. Neither was the coach. Even the cheerleaders took turns berating me. I'm not sure whether the taunts of our opponents or of my teammates were more humiliating. The result was that I never put on the uniform again. I never put on any uniform again. And I never played on another school sports team.

It was 32 years before I again tried to become an athlete. Thirty-two years later, I worked up the courage to put on a pair of running shoes and pin a race number to my chest. I had finally mustered the nerve to admit that, more than anything in my life, I'd always wanted to be an athlete.

That was my reality. I had hidden the disappointment under layers of other achievements. Even though I had a successful career, I was still living in the shadow of that shot. No amount of success, money or therapy could undo the damage. Nothing undid the damage until I put on a pair of running shoes.

lessons learned

As stupid as you think you look doing your new activity, ignore that crabby inner voice (the one telling you that your neighbours think you're nuts) and keep going. You will find that your neighbours admire your spirit, and 95 per cent of other runners are supportive of your efforts. If at all possible, gather your courage and join a local running club that is beginner-friendly. Running with the group will help you add consistency to your running, and they will be able to answer a wealth of questions about running, injuries and gear. They will also help you become accustomed to running in less desirable weather and help you get in the all-weather, year-round running habit.

– Carla Paquette, aged 33
Running for 5 years

Exorcising the Memories

What messages do you carry with you about your abilities as an athlete? The memories of the 'glory days' haunt some people. Endlessly reliving what it was like when they were in 'the best shape of their lives' keeps these people from starting over. They can't face how far they've fallen since they were at the top of their game.

Less athletically gifted people like me must erase old images, old failures and the voices that convinced us we would never be athletic. The voice may be that of a sibling, a friend or a teacher. If you listen carefully, I guarantee that you'll hear a voice telling you what your athletic potential is.

Years later, most of us still believe that voice. We still believe that our past failures predict future failures. We cling to our childhood and adolescent images as if life were a snapshot, not a motion picture. Until we exorcise the memories that keep us from succeeding, there's no point in exercising the body. It isn't the added weight on our bodies that keeps us locked in inactivity; it's the added weight on our spirits. The thought of ourselves as unathletic keeps us from becoming athletes. Our inability to imagine ourselves as runners keeps us on the sidelines.

Starting a running career or restarting an athletic career means accepting the truth about yourself. It means accepting the truth about where you are, and the distance between there and where you want to be. It means accepting that you may never achieve all of your goals. But that's no reason not to achieve some of them.

Keeping the Faith

**Staying active for a lifetime is an act of faith.
Little by little, day by day, run after run,
you'll find the answers**

The moment of truth for many of us as mature athletes is when we first realize that changing our lives is going to be much more difficult than we ever imagined. Most of us drift gently into a life of indulgence, getting out of shape so slowly that when we finally decide to turn our lives around, we're shocked to discover how far we are from where we were and where we want to be.

Most of us have lost the ability to keep the faith. We live in an age of instant gratification. We cook in seconds, eat meals in minutes and travel halfway around the world in hours. Our lives are conveniently carved into 30-minute blocks of time. We're sure that crimes can be solved, criminals punished and diseases cured in a single episode.

So, we search for shortcuts – and are surprised by our own disappointment when they don't work. We find out very quickly that the magic machine that was supposed to produce rock-hard abs with only five minutes of use a day doesn't work. We won't look like the model even if we use the machine *twice* as long as recommended, at least not without making other changes, too. The magic diet that allowed us to

34

eat as much as we wanted doesn't work. The pill that burns fat while we sleep doesn't work. In an often depressing and frightening scenario, we realize that we'll have to get back into shape one day at a time.

The Popeye Syndrome

The search for the quick solution is what I call the Popeye Syndrome. Of all the heroes on television, Popeye had the best system. When he was in trouble, all he had to do was reach into his shirt, pull out a can of spinach, squeeze it into the air, and catch the magic food in his mouth. Presto! He had instant muscles, instant strength and instant solutions. Popeye didn't have to keep the faith. He just had to remember the spinach.

No matter what Popeye had done, no matter how huge a mistake he'd made, help was only a squeeze away. Get to the spinach and you'll be fine. And so, we search for our spinach.

I wasn't quite as bright as Popeye. I thought that caffeine, alcohol and nicotine would work just as well. When I got into trouble, I reached for one of those. It kind of worked. Caffeine wired me up so that I felt stronger, alcohol made me think I was stronger, and nicotine made me worry less about how strong I was.

lessons learned

Without a doubt, I wish I had started using walk breaks from the very beginning. It would have improved my time, supported my ego and probably saved my knees a bit.

**– Pam Niebrzydowski,
aged 55
Running for 28 months**

After reading that a certain chemical would reduce my body fat, I bought it by the case. Popeye pills! It seemed much better to pop a pill than to actually monitor my food intake. If it worked for Popeye, why not me?

It didn't work because I'm not a cartoon character. Neither are you. Your progress as a runner is a frustratingly slow process of small gains. It's a matter of inching up your mileage and your pace. It's a matter of learning to celebrate the small gains as if they were Olympic victories. It means paying your dues on the road or the treadmill. It means searching for the limits of your body and demanding that your spirit not give up. It means making the most of what you have. It means making yourself an athlete one workout at a time.

I'm often asked what motivates those of us who run and walk so slowly to get out there on rainy mornings and cold afternoons. What motivates us to train, eat healthily and keep pinning on race numbers when we have no hope of winning? What motivates us to spend six months preparing for an event like the marathon when it's over in just a few hours?

The answer isn't simple. I believe that most of us discover the reason we're out there somewhere between the start line and the finish line. Whether it's our first 5-K or 25th marathon, there's always that moment of clarity when it all makes sense, that instant when we know that it's all been worth it.

I believe that because I've stood at dozens of finish lines and watched thousands of people come across. I've seen the smiles and the tears. I've heard the shouts of jubilation and the screams of triumph from those who have faced their demons and won. I've never heard anyone say that the training, the sacrifices and the hours and hours of preparation weren't worth it.

The only magic in our lives as runners is the magic of consistency. Not every run will make you feel great. Not every run will bring you to some higher level of fitness. Not every moment of every run will be filled with the joy of motion. Not every foot strike will stir your soul.

A story about a young girl who wants a pony for her birthday says it all. Her family can't afford a pony and tells her there's no way she can have one. The next morning, her father has a truckload of manure delivered so that he can fertilize his garden. When the little girl wakes up and sees the manure, she runs into the garden, grabs a shovel, and starts to dig. When asked what she's doing, she replies, 'With this much manure,

I just *know* there's a pony in there somewhere.' At times, we all feel like we're digging in the manure of our past, that the pile is bigger than we can possibly handle. We need to have that little girl's faith. We need to keep digging with hope, with the promise in our hearts that there's an active, fit person inside us somewhere. We must believe that, if we keep shovelling, our dreams will come true.

Left-brain, Right-brain Standoffs

At times, your inspiration fades, your motivation ebbs and your enthusiasm disappears. That's normal. You'll take three steps forwards and two steps back throughout your journey to a fitter, healthier lifestyle. After the first few weeks, your progress won't be linear. It's important to understand that even the bad runs are doing you some good. The days when you have to drag yourself out the door are very often the days when you will learn the most about yourself, not necessarily as a runner, but as a person.

Famous running coach, *Runner's World* magazine training expert and columnist, motivational speaker and former Olympian Jeff Galloway talks about running on the right side of your brain. The left side is the part of your brain that's rational and critical. It's the part that looks out of the window, sees rain falling and *knows* that the right thing to do is to go back to bed. The right side of your brain, on the other hand, is far less rational and more playful. The right side of your brain looks out of the window, sees rain and thinks how much fun it will be to splash through puddles. According to Galloway, the key is to trick the left side of your brain into running.

lessons learned

I never thought I could do it [run]. Even though I am 1.77 m (5 ft 10 in) and 100 kg (15½ st) I can still do it! And I can do it without pain.

– Dee Dawe, aged 36 Walking, then running since 1999

On the days when my left brain is shouting that I shouldn't run, I tell myself that I won't. I try to get my left brain to relax by agreeing with it and letting it think that it's in control. I tell myself that I'll just get into my running clothes, go outside and check out what's going on. No harm in that. No exertion, no work. I tell myself there's no way I'm going to run. I'll just walk down the street a little.

Once I'm out the door and walking, I convince my left brain to try 'jogging' a little. Not a *real* run, just a 'walk-waddle' kind of action that will propel me further from my house. I tell myself that if I get as far as the next corner, I'll turn around and go home. When I get to that next corner, I'll try going to the next, then the next … until I find myself far enough away that I might as well run to get back home. At that point, the rational left brain kicks in and agrees that as long as I'm out there, I might as well get something out of it.

At times, though, your left brain is absolutely correct. You really shouldn't run. Sometimes your right brain wants to keep playing when your left brain knows that you'll be risking injury if you do. At these times, you need to listen to the rational left side of your brain. It may be hard to

lessons learned

Even from the start, all I can remember hearing, reading and talking about was how important it was to have a good 'base'. Yes, a running base is important, but to me the truly important base was my support base.

If I had known then just how important it was to have friends and family encouraging and supporting me along the way, perhaps I would have paid more attention to them rather than obsessing about doing it right. Maybe I would have enjoyed it a little more. The it *isn't the running, the* it *is the camaraderie of meeting and making new friends and sharing this new experience with my family.*

**– Bruce Kochman, aged 47
Running off and on for 8 years**

an exercise in joy

Build faith in your ability to stick with the programmeme by learning how to listen to your body. On the days when you find yourself making excuses not to run, examine those excuses. Which side of your brain is talking? Are they merely excuses or are they real, valid points? If your knee hurts so badly that you're walking with a limp, you shouldn't run. If you're feeling down in the dumps because your pay rise wasn't as much as you expected, get out there.

believe, but at times, the best run is no run, and the best way to become a better runner is to *not* put on your running shoes. Those are the days when improvement comes from doing less rather than doing more.

It takes time to learn when to listen to which side of your brain. It may take years to understand that not running one day doesn't make you lazy or undisciplined. It may make you smart. It takes faith to believe that the days when you do nothing are as important as the days you work hard.

The minutes of being active will turn into hours, the hours into days, the days into weeks, the weeks into months and the months into years. Your memory of what it was like before you became active will dim. The person you used to be eventually becomes a stranger to you.

Staying active for a lifetime is an act of faith. It starts with a single step and continues with each step after that. The people whom you see running in your local area are no more talented than you are. They are no more highly motivated and they are no more disciplined. They haven't found a secret solution to the problems that they have to confront. They haven't been able to erase the years of inactivity in a week. The people you see running aren't any different from you or me. They're simply keeping the faith.

Basic Truths about

Getting Started

Everything you need to know to begin running with confidence and enthusiasm, including how to find the right shoes, what to wear and how to use a training plan

After reading the first four chapters, you know everything there is to know to prepare your mind for the joy of running. By now, you should feel ready to get out there. Perhaps you've already gone for your first run.

But before you continue, we need to spend some time on the nuts and bolts. Running is a simple sport that involves putting one foot in front of the other. That said, the right shoes, socks, clothes and training plan will go a long way towards enhancing your satisfaction.

You could start off as many runners do – plodding down the street at any old pace in any old outfit and wearing any old shoes. The wrong pace or distance will make you feel tired and out of breath. The wrong clothes will make running feel awkward and hot. The wrong shoes can make running feel downright painful.

The best way to inspire yourself to become a runner – and to stay a runner – is to look and act like one. That means buying the right shoes, socks and clothing to look the part. That means following a detailed training plan that will slowly prepare your body, one step at a time, to run further or faster. Here's everything you need to know.

Your Shoes

If you're going to run, you need a pair of running shoes. You would think that buying a pair would be easy. After all, you just need a left shoe and a right shoe. But it's not quite that simple.

You can get cushioned shoes, stability shoes or motion-control shoes. Then there are lightweight trainers, trail shoes and racing flats. You'll find straight lasts, curved lasts and semi-curved lasts. You'll be offered shoes with gel, shoes with air and shoes with EVA midsoles. You need one type of shoe if you overpronate, another if you supinate, and yet a different type if you have no idea *if* you pronate. It shouldn't be this hard! The days of choosing between Dunlop Green Flash and Hi Tec Squash are long gone. The days when the only decision was whether to get high-tops or low-tops are a part of yesterday.

The running shoe has become a technologically sophisticated piece of equipment. But our feet are about the same as they were in the days of the caveman. For all the advances in running shoe technology, the most important piece of equipment for us as runners is something we're born with and can't change. So before you start thinking about shoes, take off your socks and think 'feet'.

Look at them. Really look at your feet. This isn't a beauty contest; it's a study of form and function. What do you notice about your feet? What do you notice about your toes? Which little piggy is going to run long distances and which little piggy is going to be a problem?

Before you can make a preliminary decision about shoes, you have to make a best-guess judgement about the kind of feet you have. Nothing you do in the next few days or weeks is as important as learning about your feet. The time you take now can save you years of frustration and pain.

Are your feet narrow? Are they wide at the ball but narrow at the heel? Are your toes perfectly even? Does your second toe extend beyond your big toe? Have you ever broken a toe? Does one of your toes make a sharp turn at the last knuckle?

What about your toenails? Are they nice and even? Do they stick up or stick out? Are your toenails neatly trimmed or do you use them as weapons against your partner on cold nights? You need to consider these things before shopping for running shoes.

Besides the actual shape of your feet and any unusual characteristics, the two most important factors to know before shopping for shoes are your arch type and your shoe-wear pattern.

Your Arch Type

Feet fall into one of three categories: they have normal, high or low arches. It doesn't matter which you have; one isn't right or better than another for running or walking. Having a 'normal' arch doesn't mean that you'll be any more or less successful as a runner. Conversely, having high arches or flat feet doesn't spell disaster. Your arch is just a piece of the puzzle.

Luckily, it's easy enough to find out which type of feet you have by taking the 'wet foot' test. Be sure to do it with *both* feet. Spread a piece of paper on the floor. A brown paper bag that you've torn open is best, but newspaper will do. Dampen the bottom of your foot and step down lightly on the paper. What you see when you remove your foot will tell you what kind of arch you have.

The first time I tried this, I soaked my foot in water and stomped down on the paper. The result was something that looked more like a Rorschach test than an arch evaluation. Take your time. The bottom of your foot needs to be completely damp and you only need to press down hard enough to get a good impression.

What do you see? If you see a clear imprint of your heel and the ball of your foot, connected by a band along the side of your foot, you probably have a normal arch. The band along the outer edge will be continuous, but there will be a gap on the inside of your foot. The impression will look more or less like a foot.

If the imprint shows only the heel and the ball of your foot, chances are you have a high arch. The line between both the inside and the outside of your foot will be broken or very thin. You'll see dry paper in between your heel mark and the ball of your foot. If you see a giant blob that looks sort of like the entire bottom of your foot, you most likely have a low arch, or what's usually called flat feet. If you do, don't worry.

Now test the other foot. Are they the same? Do you have one flat foot and one with a high arch? It can happen. What you discover doesn't mean that you can or can't be a runner, but it will help you buy the right pair of shoes for your feet. You're still not ready to buy a pair of shoes, however. The wet foot test tells you what your foot looks like when it's static. But you're not standing in place when you run, you're moving.

lessons learned

Buy two pairs of very good shoes and alternate them every week to keep the soles from getting compressed. I was told to do that when I was having problems with shinsplints. It worked wonders!

– Amelia Pearn, aged 30
Crawling, walking, waddling, running (in that order) for 4 years

Your Shoe-wear Pattern

The way in which your foot moves through the running motion is the next piece of information you need before shopping for running shoes. Sports professionals and running specialist retailiers usually refer to this as your biomechanics. You'll learn a lot about your foot's biomechanics by looking at the shoes you already have. For now, the kind of shoes doesn't matter. Grab a pair of well-worn, flat-soled shoes and look closely at them.

Put them on a counter or tabletop so that you can see the heel at eye level. Do the shoes lean inwards or outwards? Is the heel worn on the inside or outside? Look at the wear pattern on the bottom of the soles. Are the heels wearing evenly? Is the ball of the foot showing wear across the entire width of the shoe? Do some parts of the sole look worn out while other parts look brand new?

The wear pattern of your shoes will give you clues about how your foot moves through your running stride. Most runners fit into one of three categories: neutral runners, overpronators or supinators. Again, there's no better or worse, no right or wrong. You just need to know which category fits your foot movement.

Neutral pronation. Pronation is the action of the foot rolling inwards towards the *medial* side, or middle of the foot. The biomechanically perfect or neutral foot strikes the ground near the outside of the heel and rolls slightly inwards to the inside of the ball of the foot to absorb the shock as your weight comes onto the foot. This 'ideal' movement through the action of running is said to be 'neutral'.

Overpronation. A foot whose movement exceeds the normal range is said to overpronate. The foot lands at about the right place on the heel, but as it goes through the running motion, it rolls too far inwards. The foot and your weight shift too far to the inside of the sole.

Supination. A foot that moves less than normal is said to supinate. The foot starts out at the right place on the heel, but doesn't roll inwards enough, if at all. The foot stays on the outer edge of the sole of the shoe through the entire running motion.

Most of us do not have biomechanically perfect feet. In fact, as I understand it, one person in the mid-1800s actually had such a foot. It was bronzed and preserved in a medical museum.

Your foot type and your foot movement are often, although not always, related. A low arch usually causes overpronation because the foot collapses under the weight of the body and then rolls inwards. A high arch tends to result in rigid feet that don't roll inwards enough. Neutral arches and normal movement often go hand in hand … or foot in foot.

These are general guidelines, which may vary with individual runners. For example, I have a fairly normal arch but a high instep and very flexible bones. My arch looks normal when I'm standing still, but when I run, the softness of my bones allows the arch to compress and become flat.

Don't worry if you don't get your foot evaluation right at first. You may have a high-arched left foot that supinates and a low-arched right foot that overpronates. Or you may have normal arches and low arches in motion. With so many combinations, your particular combination of foot type and motion can be tricky to pinpoint. Manufacturers of running shoes have helped *and* complicated the process.

Shoe Suede Blues

Running shoes have two main purposes. First, they're supposed to protect your foot and cushion the impact of the foot striking the ground. Second, they attempt to make your imperfect foot motion closer to the neutral ideal. Your mission is to find the combination of protection, cushioning and correction that is best suited for your foot, your running motion and your budget.

The most expensive shoe is not necessarily the best shoe for you. Bells and whistles designed to entertain you and impress your friends can drive the price of shoes up, and they won't guarantee that the shoe will work for you.

On the other hand, it's not likely that you'll find exactly the right pair of shoes for you on the clearance table. A shoe that looks like a bargain may not save you money. That 'bargain' shoe may become a doorstop if it doesn't work with your foot and your running motion.

It's an even worse idea to buy running shoes based on colour or fashion. Running shoes are essential equipment, not fashion accessories. A shoe may look great yet not work at all for you. Or, it may be the ugliest footwear you've ever seen but works perfectly.

The part of the shoe's construction that is most important is the midsole, that section of the shoe between the bottom of your foot and the ground. The midsole is where all the magic happens. Specifically, the medial (or inside) portion of the midsole is where the most important action is. Its composition and density affect the stability of the shoe and can help correct foot problems like overpronation.

Types of Shoes

The labels used to categorize running shoes seem self-descriptive and, to a certain extent, they are. Unfortunately, shoe manufacturers don't apply consistent labels within their own brands, and there is little agreement among manufacturers concerning terminology. Some generally accepted guidelines will give you a place to start.

Neutral shoes. These are the most basic, the least fancy and often the lowest-priced running shoes. They have the least amount of technology, cushioning and support. A pair of relatively inexpensive neutral shoes is a good place to start for the new runner who is uncertain of his foot type and foot movement. These shoes usually have very little or no medial support. This is visible in the midsole, which will be made entirely of the same material and will be a single colour.

Cushioned shoes. These shoes contain the manufacturer's chosen form of cushioning, ranging from air to gel to nuclear shock absorbers. Cushioning is designed to soften the impact of your foot hitting the ground with the force of $3\frac{1}{2}$ to 5 times your bodyweight. The type of cushioning you prefer is a highly individual choice.

Cushioned shoes have the softest midsole and very little medial support. They aren't designed to correct biomechanical problems; they're designed to be 'cushy'. Typically, they feel great when you're walking around the shop in them. Runners with normal arches and a neutral running motion can wear cushioned shoes. Regardless of how good a cushioned shoe may feel for the first 5 minutes, if your foot naturally moves too much or not enough, the cushioned shoe will not provide enough support and stability.

Stability shoes. Stability shoes are the bread and butter of the shoemakers. They're also the 'go-to' shoes for most shoe salespeople.

Stability shoes have decent cushioning, moderate medial support and are more durable than cushioned shoes. They seem to work best for the greatest number of runners.

The midsoles of stability shoes usually are two colours, which indicates that they're made of two densities of material. Visually, the midsole on the outer edge of the shoe is white, while the inner, or medial, side is made of a denser grey material. The grey, denser part may begin at the heel or closer to the arch of the foot. The stiffer midsole material in the medial area slows down the rate of pronation somewhat. A midpriced stability shoe is very often a good choice for the new runner who isn't sure what he wants or needs in a running shoe.

Motion-control shoes. Motion-control shoes may be the greatest innovation ever made in shoe technology. These shoes are designed to slow down or eliminate the overpronation of the foot. Without motion-control shoes, many runners who aren't blessed with perfect feet or movement would be unable to run without injury.

Motion-control shoes have the heaviest-duty medial support. In addition to a stiffer midsole material, these shoes often contain a device, usually called a medial post, to increase stability. The medial post may be a plastic bridge or a hunk of ultrahard rubber. The goal of motion-control shoes is simple: to stop the foot from rolling inwards. Happily, modern motion-control shoes are far superior to their earlier relatives, which could be stiff, heavy and very uncomfortable. Today's motion-control shoes usually include enough

lessons learned

Initially, I was wearing regular gym socks and I had blisters constantly. I had blisters on top of my old blisters! I had to wear two or three plasters on each foot every time I went running. Since I started wearing running socks, I have had two or three tiny blisters in the past year and a half.

**– Susan Bridges, aged 24
Running for 3 years**

cushioning to make them very comfortable. Motion-control shoes are often viewed as the answer for 'big' runners – people like me who began running while carrying 36 kg (5½ st) of extra weight. Although it's true that motion-control shoes can help the big runner, don't assume that because you're a large person you should wear motion-control shoes. Your feet, not your weight or size, dictate the type of shoe that's best for you.

Trail shoes. Many manufacturers are producing shoes that have been designed to wear 'off road'. These shoes are a bit heavier and often have more durable outsoles and a little more cushioning than other running shoes. Beyond the style, most of us, especially new runners, can use our regular running shoes for light trail running and modest off-road excursions.

Racing flats. I wouldn't mention racing flats, except that the first time I ran a sub-10-minute mile I went out and bought a pair. I was convinced that these lightweight shoes would make me much faster. It didn't. New runners are best advised to leave the racing flats for those

lessons learned

During my early runs, I spent far too many hours trudging along in a cotton T-shirt and beach shorts, only to arrive home with a trail of sweat on the pavement. While wringing my stuff out in the bath, my wife usually had a comment about the accompanying smell that lingered in the bathroom while they dried. She once told her sister, 'He comes in dripping wet'. It was true, I literally came in dripping wet, leaving a trail of sweat behind me. The dripping sound coming from the bathroom was not a leaky tap.

Go ahead and invest in the latest high-tech fabrics. You will notice the difference. These clothes will allow you to feel better while you run and your partner may allow you in the front door when you get back.

– James Gilcrease, aged 43
Running for 14 years

who need them. Otherwise, you'll end up like I did – an old, slow guy at the back of the pack wearing a really flashy-looking pair of shoes.

Size DOES Matter!

I didn't even try on the first pair of running shoes that I bought. I had worn size 9 shoes since secondary school. I knew what size shoe I needed. Guess what? I was wrong!

In a perfect world, running shoes wouldn't even have sizes on them. When it comes to running shoes, size is meaningless. No two manufacturers agree on what a size 9 is. A size 9 in one model of a shoe won't be the same as a size 9 in a different model by the same manufacturer, much less in a shoe by a different manufacturer!

Nine out of ten new runners buy their first pair of running shoes too small. They try them on as if they were ordinary shoes. They want them to feel snug and to fit like a glove. The fit of a running shoe is very different than other shoes you've worn. Buying a running shoe that doesn't fit right may ruin your first weeks and months of running.

A running shoe should have a thumb's width between the end of your longest toe and the end of the shoe itself. Your foot will feel like it's swimming in the toebox, but after a few miles of running, when your feet begin to swell and your toes start to rub against each other or the end of your shoes, you'll be glad to have that extra space.

Running shoes have definitely advanced since the days of rubber-soled plimsolls. Contemporary running shoes are high-tech pieces of equipment that, when matched properly to your foot, can help you run pain- and injury-free for the rest of your life. The key is matching your foot to the right (and left) shoe for you.

Your Socks

Next to your shoes, socks are your most important piece of running equipment. Like shoes, there's no right or wrong sock. Only you can decide what works best for you. Sock technology has come a long way since the days of the cotton tube sock with three stripes around the top. You'll find almost as many choices in socks as in shoes.

The first decision you'll need to make is whether to buy thick or thin socks. Are you more comfortable in a thick, heavily padded pair or a whisper-thin pair of socks? There are advantages and advocates for both. The more generous padding of some socks helps compensate for less-than-perfectly-shaped feet. The extra padding cushions and protects that little extra bump or knob on your foot. A thicker sock can also compensate for a slight difference in foot size. But some runners want the 'feel of the road' that comes only with wearing thin socks.

Regardless of their thickness, you don't want to be in the land of cotton running socks, even if you're living in the South. When your feet sweat, cotton will hold that moisture against your skin. CoolMax or other technical fabrics will draw the moisture away from your feet, keeping them dry. The drier your socks and your feet, the lower your chance of developing blisters, calluses, athlete's foot and smelly feet.

You'll need to experiment with kinds and brands of socks. You may find that one kind of sock works well for your shorter runs, but another works better as you add time and miles.

Some hard-core runners insist on running without socks. I'm not one of them. I've tried, and I can tell you that the shapes and sizes of the blisters that you can get from running sockless are infinite. With today's state-of-the-art sock technology, it's not worth the risk to run sockless.

Your Clothes

For my first run, on a day when the temperature was cool, I wore track-suit bottoms, a long-sleeved T-shirt, a sweatshirt, a jacket, gloves, and a wool watch cap. I could barely move, let alone run. Now, on the same kind of day, I'd probably go out in shorts and a long-sleeve technical shirt.

Running is a relatively inexpensive hobby. It's not like you need a £20,000 fishing boat or even a £2,000 set of golf clubs. But for the shop-til-you-drop fanatics among us, you *can* spend a lot of money on running clothes. In fact, you *should* plan to invest a little in your early running wardrobe. In the long run (pun intended), it will be money well spent.

You know you're a runner when you start using words like CoolMax, Dri-Line, and Dri-Fit as part of your daily vocabulary. You know you're an informed runner when the mere thought of running in a cotton T-shirt sounds as sensible to you as putting your shoes on the wrong feet.

Whatever the brand name, all of the contemporary technical fabrics are designed to move moisture *away* from your body. Keeping your

Inspirational
Tools of the Trade

Before moving on to Part 2, make sure you have:

1. Bought a pair of running shoes
2. Bought a new pair of non-cotton running socks
3. Bought a running outfit
4. Obtained your doctor's blessing
5. Studied your training plan
6. Read and completed 'An Exercise in Joy' in each chapter

body dry means that it will stay warmer in cold weather and cooler in the heat. Moving sweat away from your skin and into the atmosphere is your running garment's most important job.

The well-dressed new runner's wardrobe will include:

- ► A couple of pairs of running shorts (the classic loose-fitting shorts with an attached liner, or the skin-tight 'bicycle'-style shorts, without the padding)
- ► A pair of synthetic-fibre tights
- ► A couple of short-sleeved and long-sleeved technical shirts
- ► A lightweight, water-resistant running jacket

You'll be able to run in almost every weather condition by mixing and matching these wardrobe basics.

Don't despair if you live and want to run in harsher, colder climates. There's a running garment that will keep you warm and dry in the severest weather conditions, including bone-chilling sub-zero temperatures and gale-force winds. Very few excuses, except possibly the presence of flood or lightning, need to keep you from running.

Your 12-week Training Plan

You have shoes that are two sizes bigger than your brother's, socks that cost more than a bottle of wine, and running clothes that draw sweat into the outer atmosphere. You're ready for your first run. But first, as with any exercise programme, you should consult your doctor if you have any doubts about whether it's safe for you to proceed.

There are lots of training programmes for the new runner. The 'getting started' programme that is described here is the one I've used most successfully with mature athletes like myself. I've received so much positive feedback about it that I'm sure most new runners can use it.

This is a 'from the sofa to the start line' programme. It's based on the amount of time you spend on your feet, not on the mileage you run. It assumes that you have no aerobic base whatsoever. You can start this programme with hope and finish it with pride.

This programme has no instructions for *what* activity to do. It just indicates *how long* you should do it. That means you can run a little, walk some way or stroll a while. Just be active. The most important part of a new programme of activity is to start gently and be patient. This is, after all, just the first 12 weeks of your new life of activity.

The next section of this book will discuss the elements of training: mode, intensity, duration and frequency. But for now, the most important element is that you get started. Try to keep your expectations reasonable. You're beginning the journey of a thousand miles with a single step. Each step is important; every step counts. Here are some early week-by-week pointers for using your training plan.

Week 1. Don't try to run at all the first week. You may be tempted, but use your athletic discipline and don't run. It's enough to get off the sofa and out of your house during the first week. Walk around your local area or the shops. What you do and where you do it doesn't matter. Eventually, you'll mix in some running, but not too much and not too soon.

Week 2. Try running for 30 seconds for every 5 minutes of walking. Try not to feel frustrated or anxious about the amount of time you spend walking. Even now, 10 years after *my* first running steps, I include regular walking breaks in many of my runs.

The ratio of running to walking changes from running 4 minutes and walking 1 minute, to running 5 minutes and walking 1 minute, depending on how I feel. The walk break, as advocated by Jeff Galloway, is an integral part of this programme, too.

lessons learned

It is a must to go to a running shop and get fitted for your first pair of shoes. And don't let CoolMax be a secret that you find out about after you start chafing. Two other essentials:

- *Vaseline or Body Glide for chub rub*

- *Rub deodorant on your feet to prevent blisters. I didn't do that until my sixth marathon, and I wish I had done for the first five!*

**– Elizabeth Itter, aged 36
Running for 4½ years**

WEEK	SESSIONS (TICK OFF EACH ONE)			SESSIONS PER WEEK	TIME PER DAY	TOTAL TIME FOR WEEK
1	☐	☐	☐	3	20 min	60 min
2	☐	☐	☐	3	20 min	60 min
3	☐	☐	☐	3	25 min	1 hr 15 min
4	☐	☐	☐	3	25 min	1 hr 15 min
5	☐	☐	☐	3	30 min	1 hr 30 min
6	☐	☐	☐ ☐	4	25 min	1 hr 40 min
7	☐	☐	☐ ☐	4	25 min	1 hr 40 min
8	☐	☐	☐ ☐	4	30 min	2 hr
9	☐	☐	☐ ☐	4	30 min	2 hr
10	☐	☐	☐ ☐	4	3 × 30 min 1 × 45 min	2 hr 15 min
11	☐	☐	☐ ☐	4	3 × 30 min 1 × 45 min	2 hr 15 min
12	☐	☐	☐ ☐	4	3 × 35 min 1 × 45 min	2 hr 30 min

Week 3. If you're comfortable with the activity level, try running 1 minute every 5 minutes. But no more!

Week 4 and beyond. Little by little, week by week, increase the time you run and decrease the time you walk. By the 6th week of the programme, you should be walking and running in nearly equal amounts of time. Continue to alternate between the two, but spend the same amount of time doing each. By the 12th week, your goal should be to run for 5 minutes and then walk for 1 minute.

The fun and satisfying part of this programme is making the transition from mostly walking with a little running to mostly running with a little walking; remember, however, that there's no absolute sequence. If you find that you're out of breath at the end of the running section, don't run so long or so fast.

This programme is designed to help you break free from sedentary confinement. It shouldn't hurt, you shouldn't be in pain, and most of all, you shouldn't *hate* it. Don't run or walk so fast that you get winded or so slow that you get bored. Find the point of balance between wanting to keep going and wanting to give up.

And DON'T do more than is recommended. You won't get bonus points for overtraining in the first few weeks of this programme. For now, just take it easy, enjoy yourself and learn to find satisfaction in moving your body. And please, tick off your training sessions as you do them. Twelve weeks from now, you'll be amazed at how much you've accomplished!

Recommended Reading

► Burfoot, Amby. *The Principles of Running: Practical Lessons from My First 100,000 Miles*. Emmaus, PA: Rodale Inc., 1999.

► Galloway, Jeff. *Galloway's Book on Running*. Bolinas, CA: Shelter Publications, 1984.

► Jerome, John. *The Elements of Effort: Reflections on the Art and Science of Running*. New York, NY: Breakaway Books, 1997.

► Kowalchik, Claire. *The Complete Book of Running for Women: Everything You Need to Know about Training, Nutrition, Injury Prevention, Motivation, Racing and Much, Much More*. New York, NY: Pocket Books, 1999.

► Sheehan, George. *Running and Being: The Total Experience*. New York, NY: Simon and Schuster, 1978.

► Will-Weber, Mark. *The Quotable Runner: Great Moments of Wisdom, Inspiration, Wrongheadedness, and Humor*. New York, NY: Breakaway Books, 1995.

Part 2
Perspiration

Our Bodies, Our Selves

You can't trade in your body for a new, improved model. Accepting the natural strengths and weaknesses of the body you have is the key to becoming the best you can be

Many mature-beginner athletes believe that living an active lifestyle would be easier if they could trade the body they have for the body they want. I did. Part of my continuing fantasy was finding a training programme that would alter the essential features of my body. The fantasy was that the programme would alter my body *before* I did any perspiring.

If my legs were just a little longer, my shoulders a little broader and my waist a little narrower, I would have had a head start on at least *looking* fit. I thought that if I could look fit first, I would be more motivated to actually get fit. Like many overweight people, I assumed that if I were thin, I would be fit. That's why for me, every new fitness regime began with dieting. I wasn't ready to start moving the body I had. I wanted to get it down to a size and shape that was easier to move. Looking back, it's no wonder that I hated the idea of exercising. To me, exercising meant first giving up all the foods I liked.

I once chastised a music student for not practising, and she replied that when she got good enough, she'd start practising. I tried to explain that it didn't work that way. She simply shrugged and walked away. In fact, I was no more aware than that student. I was waiting until I got into shape before I got into shape. I never put the two elements together.

Until I started running, I never understood that the shape, form, weight, strength and fitness level of my body were the result of the perspiration, not the diet. I viewed my body like wrapping paper. My body hid what was inside so that no one could guess the contents. No one could see what the smoking was doing to my lungs. No one could see what the drinking was doing to my liver. No one could see what the poor food choices were doing to my arteries.

Of course, it's much easier to get thin than to get fit. Getting thinner is simply a matter of denying yourself nourishment for as long as you can. If you reduce your caloric intake enough, your body will begin to devour itself, and in a few weeks or months, you'll be thinner. But you won't be fit. In fact, it's likely that you'll be in worse shape

lessons learned

The thought of running had always intimidated me. I saw runners as superhuman athletes who had become masters of their bodies, and I was scared to enter that arena and run among the lions. What I've learned is that the running community is one of the most compassionate, giving, understanding and supportive communities I've ever been involved in. I've realized that even the best of runners have been humbled by bad days, that we all need encouragement, and that we ultimately have the same goal: to keep moving. Had I known that other runners would accept what limited abilities I had when I first began running, that they would encourage me every step of the way, that so many of them started out like I had, and that I really could reach my goals, I would have put on my running shoes a lot earlier in life.

– James Connell, aged 32
Running for 2 years

than before you lost weight. Fitness requires perspiration. There's no shortcut around that fact.

My Legs Are Too Short: Excuses for Being Unfit

I'm not sure where we get the ideas we have about our bodies. I've heard people complain about the images in the media, the cocaine-addict look of models and the you-can-never-be-too-rich-or-too-skinny way of thinking. I suppose that contributes, but I suspect that most body image problems go back further than the latest fashion magazine.

For me, it started as a youngster shopping for trousers with a little more room in the seat and a little less length in the legs. I had the impression that somehow my legs weren't quite what they ought to be. At least, they weren't what I wanted them to be.

This gave me a convenient excuse when I was unable to achieve my athletic goals as a youngster. If I wasn't as fast as the other children, couldn't jump as high, or hit the ball as far, it was because my legs were too short. Eventually, I gave up on athletics. What was the point? I would never be able to overcome my genetic deficiencies.

So I began an active life on legs that I was sure were too short. Too short for what, I didn't know – they were just too short. I only knew, or believed, that whatever it was, my legs were too short.

For me, it was legs. For others, it's a stomach that's too big or hips that are too wide. I've talked to people who aren't active because they have bad feet, bad knees, funny toes or floppy ears. It doesn't matter what part of your body you belittle. Chances are you've found the part that allows you to excuse yourself from being more active.

I say this because I've met people who have really bad knees but have learned how to be prudent in their training. And they've accomplished all of their running goals! The key is learning to train and perspire sensibly. Too often, the problem *isn't* our bodies. It's our stubborn refusal to take the bodies we have into consideration when we start to get more active.

Transforming your sedentary adult body into a tool that you can use to achieve your athletic dreams takes more patience than discipline, more tenacity than talent. It takes learning to respect both the features and functions of your body.

No Pain, No Gain: How Not to Justify Abusing Your Body

I learned to respect my body the hard way – by abusing it. In my pre-running life, I abused it with smoking, drinking, overeating and pushing myself to extremes. I expected my body to forgive me for asking it to go beyond itself and to forget about the damage I was doing to it. I expected my body to recover from the abuse without any help from me.

Lying on a trolley in an emergency unit, hooked up to an ECG machine, hearing the doctor tell my wife that my blood pressure was 185 over 130 had no effect on me whatsoever. I was only 28 years old. Surely, it was too soon to have to start worrying about things like high blood pressure. The pain in my chest seemed a small price to pay for the fun I was having.

Fifteen years later, when I started to become more active, I took the same gung-ho attitude into my running. I was sure that my body would react differently to the stresses of training than other people's bodies did. If the 'normal' body needed to rest three days a week, my body needed only 1 day. If the 'normal' body could handle increasing mileage by 10 per cent per week, I was sure that *mine* could handle a 30 per cent increase.

I transferred my abusive attitude to an activity that was more acceptable. I took pride in the aches and pains I was creating in my body. I abused my body by overtraining. The more I limped around on battered joints, the more I felt like an athlete. In those days, we joked that if I were in any better shape, I wouldn't be able to walk at all.

I'm not alone in this. Walk through the field lined up at any local 10-K and you'll think you're at an orthopaedic convention. You'll hear

an exercise in joy

Think back to the excuses you've used to not be an athlete. What have you blamed on your body? Do you have knock-knees, flat feet, small feet or huge feet? Do you have a slow metabolism or a slow pace? Whatever excuses you've used, none of them will prevent you from perspiring to the best of your individual potential. If you experience pain while running, you most likely can solve it by buying the right shoes or seeing a chiropodist or a physiotherapist for corrective exercises. Remember: no pain, all gain.

about every imaginable physical impairment and see every imaginable contrivance for keeping a body together. You'll see tape, elastic bandages, splints and tubes wrapped around every conceivable part of the runners' bodies. Like I did, these injured runners seem to take pride in the fact that they are 'playing with pain'. They've convinced themselves that the tape and tubes are medals of honour.

Have you ever seen a runner in the lead pack of a major marathon wearing a knee brace? Have you *ever*? Of course not. Elite runners know better. They know that their bodies are their primary assets. They're not going to risk a permanent injury to finish one race.

Using – Not Abusing – the Body You Have

The truth is that, as adults, many of us are convinced we could be and do all that we want if only we had the right body. We spend our lives living in the darkness of what we could have been. Like the boxer in *On the Waterfront*, we believe that with the right body, we 'could have been a contender'. Unfortunately, the only way to make sure that you get the body you want is to be very careful when picking your parents. Genetics may not be the only criterion, but it's an important one that we can't overcome as adults.

At one race, I was doing my pre-race warmup near Bill Rodgers, who won both the Boston and New York marathons four times each. I couldn't help smiling as I watched him. All the evidence I needed to explain why he is who he is and why I am who I am was right there in front of me. He looked like an antelope as he warmed up. Everything about his body was right. The way his feet were connected to his ankles, his ankles to his legs and his legs to his hips was exactly the way you would design the body of a marathon runner. I bet he hasn't had any body fat since he was six months old.

As I looked down and compared his body to my body, I thought, 'Good grief!' All the parts had the same names, but they surely didn't have the same look. I suppose I should have been upset, but I just had to laugh. How strange, I thought, that in a few minutes, he and I would be lining up together.

It's very difficult for us as adults to accept that someone with essentially the same body we have has achieved every athletic accomplishment on record. Olympic athletes don't have an extra lung to help them breathe. They may have a gift, they may have talent, they may have the training, but they don't have anything *extra*. When we accept that the bodies of those more physically gifted are fundamentally no different than ours, we can begin to accept and understand that our bodies react to training in exactly the same way that theirs do.

This point was emphasized to me one evening when I had dinner with Khalid Khannouchi, who broke the world record for the marathon in 1999. He and I ran the same marathon in Chicago on the same course on the same day. He finished in 2:05:42. I finished in just over 5:30:00. In fact, I heard the announcement that he had set the world's record as I was approaching mile 11 of the racecourse! As we talked about our preparation and training – the tempo runs, the speedwork, the long runs – it became clear that we were talking about the same things. The difference wasn't in the content or quality of the workouts, it was only in the speed at which we were running them. Speed was the variable. Effort was the constant. Our bodies react the same way to stress and recovery. What feels like an all-out effort to a world record holder feels the same to someone at the back of the pack.

Accepting this truth about my body was one of the first steps towards making genuine progress as a runner. Accepting the truth that no body can do more than 100 per cent was a revelation to me. My best was my best. I could train hard, smart and with intensity and purpose. The only thing that would change was what my best would be. My best would never be Khannouchi's or anyone else's best.

It finally clicked that as flawed, fragile and out of shape as I had allowed my body to become, it was still the body that I was going to have to use. I couldn't trade it in for a new, improved one. I was going to get where I wanted to be in *this* body, with *these* feet. That's true for you, too. It isn't a matter of getting the body you want, it's a matter of doing the most you can with the body you have.

lessons learned

When I started running, I was tense, thinking this would help me go faster. Tense muscles, tense arms, teeth clamped firmly in place. I was determined to be good at this! Once someone told me to keep my shoulders relaxed, my hands loose and my face relaxed, I got longer, better-quality runs. I also realized that faster is not better.

– Cathy Hull, aged 53 Running for 2 years

This revelation made all the difference for me, and I think it will for you, too. You may never become *the* best, but you can become *your* best. You can find ways to improve for the rest of your life. You can find new challenges and new means for expressing your athleticism. You just have to learn to do all these new things with your old body.

Method or Madness

Master these four keys of training, and you'll never think you need to 'try harder' again!

From the time we were children, we were led to believe that the way to get better at anything from schoolwork and jobs to relationships and athletics was to try harder. For most of my life I was convinced that the reason I failed at *anything* was because I hadn't tried hard enough.

The not-trying-hard-enough mentality is exactly what gets many new runners into trouble. My first attempt at running – that wheezing, flailing, stumbling jaunt down my street – should have been enough to convince me that I was terribly out of shape and that it would take months, if not years, to become a runner. But it didn't.

I thought I wasn't trying hard enough. I thought I could overcome the damage I had done to my body with effort. I thought it was effort – just trying harder – that would lead me to my goal. Looking back, I see how misguided that idea was, but at the time, it made all the sense in the world. It never occurred to me that solid, carefully planned and executed training was the key to improvement.

Many new runners believe that it's effort that separates them from the élite, from those who are winning trophies, and even from those who are in front of them at races. They believe that if we just dig deep enough, we should be able to pass the entire field and win the race or beat our particular age group.

And why wouldn't you think that effort was the only measure of performance? Didn't you think you could have got an 'A' on the maths test if you had only tried harder? Didn't you think you would have been given a bigger pay rise if you had only tried harder? Didn't you think that the relationship you lost would have worked if only you had tried harder?

If we're honest with ourselves, we can find plenty of instances when we beat ourselves up because we didn't try hard enough. It may be that trying harder would have helped in some cases, but not always. Trying harder doesn't always equal more success; it leads to more frustration, less satisfaction and giving up.

The greatest danger we face as mature athletes is taking this 'try harder' approach into our new, active lives. We are in for trouble if we believe that if running 3 days a week is good, then 5 days a week must be better, or that if going a mile a day is good, then 2 miles a day must be twice as good. This approach often leads to frustration, injury, burnout and failure. The good news is that it can be avoided!

The Basics of Effort-based Training

As new athletes, you need to learn what every successful athlete knows: that an effective lifetime programme of activity requires finding a balance in your training.

Whether you're in your first week of activity or have been a lifelong athlete, the means to improvement boil down to four fundamental elements: mode, intensity, duration and frequency. Understanding these elements and their effects on your body in training can mean the difference between success and failure. If you have too much or too little of any of the elements, a groove can become a rut.

Being successful and achieving your goals depends on finding the right combination of mode, intensity, duration and frequency for you. In other words, you must find the best mixture of the type of training you're going to do, how difficult that training is going to be, how long you're going to do it and how often you'll do it. It's simple when you break it down into each component.

Mode. At first, this means asking yourself what you're going to do to get to where you want to be. This book is about running, but that's not to say that running is the only way to get fitter. In fact, for many new runners, running can't be the only way. Our bodies won't tolerate the pounding of a fitness programme that focuses exclusively on running.

Remember that your heart and lungs don't care how you improve your cardiovascular system, they only care that you do. Your lungs need to learn to suck more oxygen and to get that oxygen into your bloodstream. Then your heart needs to get stronger so it can pump that blood to the muscles that need it. In a sense, you need to think of your cardiovascular system as an independent component of your overall fitness. Your ability to run will be improved by a more efficient oxygen delivery system, but running isn't the only way to build that efficiency. And your running isn't the only beneficiary of an improved cardiovascular system.

Although your heart and lungs may not care how they get stronger or what mode of activity you use, your muscles and joints *do* care – a lot. Your muscles are the first element of activity that will have to make some changes. Muscles are very specific and very conservative when it comes to change.

If, like me, you have been overweight and inactive for years, your muscles have adapted to that. I spent hours watching television and drinking beer. The muscles required for me to watch television and drink beer became very highly developed. It was possible for me to remain seated and drink for 8, 10 and even 12 hours without worrying about any kind of muscle fatigue. I don't recall a time when I had to back off this activity because my muscles had reached their limit. In fact, there were times when I was able to really push myself to sit and drink for days without a hint of muscle cramping.

There was no wall for me to hit because I had slowly, carefully and relentlessly trained my sitting and drinking muscles. I could lift a bottle or glass to my mouth hundreds of times in the course of a football game and not hit the wall. My muscles didn't make judgements. They just got better at what I was asking them to do.

One of the great features of our muscles and joints is that they'll tell us that doing the same thing over and over is not a good idea. Our bodies don't often surprise us. The early-warning system of overuse is gentle, but it's always there. It begins as an ache, makes its way to a pain, and only later becomes an injury. In the process of moving from ache to pain to injury we ignore all the signs – the soreness, stiffness or inflammation. We pretend to be blind and deaf to the sounds of our bodies telling us to take it easy.

So mode becomes a very important part of your new running programme You can avoid most overuse problems by changing modes, by choosing a different set of complementary activities. You do that by cross-training. Ride a bicycle. Join a gym. Get in the pool. It doesn't matter. Do something that works your heart and lungs but uses different muscles and joints than those used in running. For example, you might run three days a week and cycle or swim three days a week.

Intensity. Intensity is the amount of stress you put on your body. Most new athletes fall victim to the 'no pain, no gain' mentality and go at every workout as if the fate of the free world depends on the results. It's that 'try harder' syndrome again. You have to fight against it all the time!

lessons learned

I wish someone had told me that I would not feel like a runner overnight. Believe me, I tried. I did too much and went too fast, too often. I ended up injured and worse – down in the dumps because I could not see myself as a runner. Not until reading lots of books did I realize that it would take time to achieve that vision.

– Cecelia Ortega, aged 47
Running for 3 years

I was convinced that the way to become a faster runner was to try to run fast all the time. The logic was compelling: in order to run fast, you must run fast. How much more straightforward could it be? When a coach first told me that the way I was going to get faster was by slowing down, I looked at him in disbelief. 'Wait a minute,' I thought. 'People are paying this man good money to tell them things that don't make any sense. I want that job!'

'To get faster, slow down.' I repeated that mantra over and over in my head, but I couldn't make myself believe it. To go slower, you go slower. To go faster, you go faster! How could it be any other way?

This is how. Your body gets stronger during the process of stress and recovery. Both words are important. The balance between the two is critical. Too much stress, and your body breaks down. Not enough recovery, and your body isn't ready for the next level of stress.

The training effect occurs during the recovery phase. Only when the body is healing itself does it become stronger, more fit and in better shape. Without adequate recovery time, your body will not become stronger. Without recovery, it will never be more than it is right now.

Of course, I didn't believe a word of this at first. If you're thinking, 'OK, that may be true for everyone else, but not for me!' I understand; I was the same way. I limped around for the better part of a year. I *over-trained* every part of my body that I trained. I really believed I was get-ting into better shape – that the soreness, the stiffness, the injuries were a necessary part of the process.

But my running became stagnant. My progress, which had been linear and pretty astonishing until then, came to a screeching halt. Because I was getting slower and slower, I trained harder and harder until I was so overtrained that my body finally broke down.

What successful athletes know that I didn't know is that the only way to be prepared to do the intense workouts with the intensity they require is to allow your body to relax and recover at other times. You do that by mixing together very easy, moderate and very intense training sessions. For example, on Monday, you might run hard and fast. On Tuesday, you take the day off or run slowly and easily.

an
exercise
in **joy**

Before going any further, think about and decide on what is the best mode, intensity, duration and frequency for you.

Mode: What else will you mix in with running?

Intensity: How much do you want to push yourself? One intense workout a week is plenty for a beginner.

Duration: How far do you want to run? Attempt your longest run only once a week.

Frequency: Which days will you run and which days will you cross-train? In the beginning, try to either cross-train or rest after every running day.

Duration. There is an inverse relationship between duration and intensity. The longer any exercise session is, the lower the intensity should be. On the other hand, the more intense the session, the shorter the duration of the workout. The key is that only you can define long and short as well as hard and easy.

A short but intense training session may be 1 hour long for a veteran, competitive marathon runner. For a new runner, a short but intense training sequence may last for 10 seconds. For both runners, the definition changes over time. It is finding this connection between duration and intensity that causes problems for runners at any level.

How long is a long time? That's like asking how old is old. I don't have the answer. I do know, however, that any training programme that attaches a time requirement to intensity workouts is a recipe for disaster. Each of us can maintain an effort level of about half our maximum perceived effort almost indefinitely, regardless of what that perceived effort level is. We may not be able to maintain it continuously, but with a few exceptions, most of us can move our bodies at about half of our perceived maximum for as long as we want.

That level of effort may be walking around the shopping centre or an amusement park. The lowest point of perceived effort is the feeling that you are not exactly sitting still, that you can do this for a long time, but that at some point, you're going to be glad to stop.

Initially, moving to a higher level of fitness means moving up a little on the scale of perceived effort. Getting into better cardiovascular condition means working those systems at a higher rate than rest for some period of time. It means requiring your entire body to do more than it's accustomed to doing, and doing it for a bit longer than it wants.

The other end of the duration scale is asking your body to do a whole lot more than it's accustomed to, but asking that it do so only for a very short period of time. Very short, intense effort can yield great results if it's done with caution.

At first, my body could sustain these intense bursts of effort for about 20 seconds. Twenty seconds may not seem like very long, but I can assure you that 20 seconds of serious effort can be an eternity. This short, intense effort is not likely to have a direct benefit to the cardiovascular system that is responding so well to the longer, less intense efforts. It's not intended to. The short-duration efforts are designed to work a very specific group of muscles, like those that improve leg speed or foot turnover.

If you ask your body to do a little more for a little longer, chances are good that your body will cooperate. But new athletes often try to get what they think is the maximum benefit out of a workout by combining the benefits of increased effort with increased duration. They ask their bodies to do a lot more for a lot longer – with disastrous results.

Finding the balance between being too intense for too long or not intense enough for too short a time is the key to a successful training programme. If your workouts are too intense for too long, you'll probably develop an injury. If your workouts are too short at a low level of intensity, you'll never achieve your goals.

Frequency. How much is enough? How much is too much? What's the maximum you can do with the minimum risk? What is the most you can do without reaching the point where you can't do any more? These are the questions that have plagued new athletes since the beginning of time.

When I buy something, I want the maximum quality at the minimum price. But I often get the minimum acceptable quality at the maximum acceptable price because there isn't always a direct correlation between the quality I want and the price I can afford. The result is that I have to work out what level of quality I'll accept at the price I can pay.

It's not that different for the new athlete. You want to get in better shape. You want to make changes in your level of activity, your eating habits and maybe some other lifestyle areas. But you can't change everything and become a fit, healthy, thin, world-class athlete by a week from Tuesday. Most of our lives, as well as our bodies, will accommodate only a limited amount of change at any given moment. Don't misunderstand – I didn't learn this the easy way. I learned it by making dramatic changes that I couldn't sustain and then giving up.

If you want to start a running programme, the first question to ask is how often you think you'll be able to run. Forget about the programmes that tell you to exercise 7 days a week. Forget about the programmes that require 12 hours of workout time a day. You must decide what kind of time and what level of frequency you have time for. Be clearheaded and

lessons learned

Take it slow. It is so easy to rush into running and to try to conquer every distance from the 5-K to the marathon during your first year of running. This can lead to injuries, burnout and missing out on the 'process' of becoming a runner. There is so much to enjoy along the way, from improved fitness to better health to higher self-confidence. Instead of rushing this process or hurrying it along, take it slow and enjoy each step along the way. Pretty soon, you will have that experience and you will be the one others look to for advice. Until then, take time to enjoy each new experience that comes your way and enjoy becoming an athlete.

– Jen Surowiecki, aged 28
Been running off and on most of my life but running became a 'real' part of my life and something that I enjoyed during the summer of 1996

realistic. Forget about the idea that you can do something for five minutes a day and achieve your fitness dreams. That won't work, either.

As a beginning mature athlete, three days a week of any kind of
activity is usually all our bodies can handle. Most of us need both physical and emotional rest days to recover from a three-day week of
activity. Is there something magic about three days a week? Sort of ...
but it's not absolute.

Doing something once a week is better than doing nothing at all.
Don't use having limited time as an excuse to do nothing. If your life
and schedule allow you to train by walking or running for 30 minutes
only once a week, then by all means get out there and do that.

But consider the other elements of mode, intensity, and duration.
One workout a week doesn't give you enough days to have a balanced
programme. Twice a week is better, especially if those days are far
enough apart to allow for recovery. You'll get benefits, although somewhat limited ones, from a twice-a-week programme.

The greatest fitness benefits occur with a programme of three days
of activity. Three days allows you to mix and match both intensity and
duration, and to include a variety of modes. Three days allows for a
short, intense workout; a long, easy workout; and something in the
middle. The magic of three days is that you can include everything.

After three days, you reach the point of diminishing returns. You
won't get 25 per cent more improvement in any area by adding a
fourth day. A fourth day will do you some good, but the line of
improvement begins to flatten out. By the time you reach the fifth and
sixth days, the line of improvement is almost horizontal.

Don't try to calculate, as I did, that you can run three days, bike
three days, swim three days, row three days, lift three days, and on and
on. It doesn't quite work that way. The various systems (cardiovascular,
musculoskeletal) begin to overlap. Then it *does* get complicated.

For now, what's important is finding the frequency that gives you
maximum improvement with minimum risk – the frequency that will
take you closer to your goal without driving you out of your mind. The
four elements – mode, intensity, duration, and frequency – are the ingredients for your own personal magic potion for an active, healthy lifestyle.

Rubbish In, Rubbish Out

Eating the wrong foods will keep you chained to the sofa, but if you can 'see' the food on your plate, you'll feel more like running

Ask almost anyone why they want to be more active and, if they're honest, they'll tell you they want to lose weight. They may couch it in language like 'toning up' or 'getting in shape', but what most of us really mean is 'skinnier'. Given all the evidence to the contrary, we're convinced that fit equals thin, and thin equals healthy.

Runners know better. At least the runners at the back of the pack know better. I long ago gave up trying to predict how fast someone is by the shape of his or her body. Men and women whose bodies were clearly built more for comfort than for speed have hammered me. I've worked with enough adult athletes to know that an extra pound or so, a little cellulite here and there, and a bit of a tummy can be found on some exceedingly fit people.

But most adults, especially those of us who have fought a losing battle with diets all of our lives, expect activity to be a magic bullet. We're sure that all we need to do is get out and move around a little and the weight will begin to fall off. We desperately want to believe that activity will overcome all of our bad habits.

Nowhere is this truer than in marathon training programmes. It must be written somewhere that all marathon runners are skinny little people with tiny waists and tight buttocks. I'm convinced that there's a secret book with an artist's rendition of what runners look like after training for six months that's passed around among potential first-time marathon runners.

That image is pure fantasy. It takes me more than five hours to run a marathon. During that time, I burn about 2,600 calories. Trust me, those lost 2,600 calories are back in about four minutes if I get to a fast-food place that serves hot-fudge sundaes. It's much easier to get calories in than to get weight off.

Food as Fuel

It's true that being more active can help with weight loss and weight management, but only as part of an overall programme of increased activity *and* better food choices. Understanding that your body has to do something with the food you eat and learning how your body uses food as fuel is an important step in gaining control over what you put into your body.

Most of us are much more careful about the quality of the fuel we put into our cars than we are about the fuel we put into our bodies. We want our cars to be fuel-efficient and our appliances to be energy-efficient, but we want our bodies to digest and burn up whatever we feel like putting into them.

The chips and beer that taste so good, that piece of pie you can't resist and the extra scoop of ice cream have to go somewhere once they enter your body. They must be processed into fuel for your muscles, your brain and your chemical and emotional systems. That truth escapes more than a few of us. It escaped me.

I once dabbled in the designer drug business. It was all legal, of course. I mixed up a batch of nicotine, caffeine, sugar and alcohol every day. Sometimes I'd take them individually. Sometimes I'd take them all together. The plan was to get to the point where they all balanced out and I was feeling good.

My biggest problem was that I wasn't a very good scientist. If I drank enough caffeine to get a buzz, I'd smoke an extra cigarette or two in order to settle down. If I became high on sugar, I'd drink a beer (or 12) to calm down. In almost 40 years, I never got it right.

For me, and for most new athletes, the first step in gaining control over our food choices is accepting that food is fuel. Food is the ingredient your body uses to keep running and to heal, rebuild and improve itself. Without the right fuel and the right mixture of ingredients, very little will change.

For most of my life I didn't view food as fuel. I didn't even think of food as *food*. Food was comfort. Food was love. Food was companionship. In my case, chocolate was comfort, pasta was love and popcorn with lots of butter was companionship. Actually, chocolate was also love. Wait, chocolate was also companionship. In fact, chocolate was love, hope, charity, truth, justice and a natural right!

I was a recreational eater. All forms of recreation provided opportunities for me to eat. Go to a movie: eat. Go to a football match: eat. Go to the motorcycle races: eat. Party? Eat. Meeting? Eat. Go out to eat. EAT!

Diets: Nobody's Right if Everybody's Wrong

I can't think of anything about which there is more controversy than dieting and food. You can barely get through a week without reading or hearing about some new discovery that contradicts the discovery that was announced the week before. Every one of them is a breakthrough. And every one of them makes it more and more difficult to know what to do.

Pick a programme – high carbohydrates, low carbohydrates, no carbohydrates. High protein, low protein. Low fat, no fat. How can you begin to make sense out of all of these contradictory 'truths'? You can't. So don't try. Remember, nobody's right if everybody's wrong.

There. I said it. You can't make sense out of the contradictory 'facts' about dieting. If you try, you'll end up going back and forth between programmes that are absolutist in nature. You'll spend the rest of your life serially eliminating certain foods from your diet. When it comes to eating, the only real insanity you need to stop is your own.

So what should you do? Let's start with what not to do. There is no way you will be successful if you stop eating everything you like today, start eating everything you hate tomorrow, and tell yourself that you'll stick with this plan for the rest of your life. I know; I tried it. Not once, but about 30 times, usually starting in early January. Almost every year, my resolution was to eliminate everything I liked to eat from my diet. My resolve usually lasted about five days.

You won't do it either, because it isn't the right thing to do. You won't stick with any eating regime that requires you to either 1. eat only foods that you can't stand or 2. stop eating all the foods that you enjoy. You also won't be successful on a programme that allows you to eat as much as you want of everything you like. It's like the level of activity that we talked about in the previous chapter. Eating well for life is a matter of balance.

The 'See-food' Diet

The simplest place to begin is with what I call the see-food diet. This came to me one evening as I was going along a restaurant buffet queue when I realized that every menu item I chose was offered to me with something covering it. I was asked if I wanted gravy on the meat, sour cream on the potato and cheese sauce on the broccoli! The best, though, was when I ordered spaghetti and asked for the sauce 'on the side'. I was presented with a very nice plate of pasta and a bowl of sauce big enough to swim in.

So I started making sure that when I ate, I could actually *see* my food. There's nothing inherently wrong with a serving of meat, a potato and a vegetable. There *is* something inherently wrong with the same servings of food buried beneath a flood of gravy, sour cream and melted cheese.

Once I started to see my food, I was surprised at how often people tried to hide food from me. The food was always covered, with everything from 'special sauces' to 'delicious toppings'. More interesting, when I asked that the special sauce or topping be left off, the waiters took offence. They seemed to be worried that if I could see my food, I might also be able to taste it.

There are no 'rules to eat by', but there are some guidelines that may help you decide not only what but also how much of it to put into your body.

Make quality carbohydrates the cornerstone of your diet. Carbs. Carbos. Carbo-loading. Sounds cool, doesn't it? Athletes have to have those carbs. Do you? Yes and no.

lessons learned

The one thing I wish I had known when I started running is just how important water is to your body. Without proper hydration, there are so many variables that can come into play, especially where the summers are HOT!

– Brian Spradley, aged 36 Running for 2½ years

Carbohydrates are the fast-burning fuel. They are the petrol-style fuel that goes into your system fast. All you need to do is light them up and watch them burn. Carbs feel good going in and even better while they're burning. Carbohydrates are not the enemy. They are also not a magic bullet. They are just a type of fuel with specific properties to which your body reacts in predictable ways. Foods high in carbohydrates are high in sugars as well. Sugar is a carbohydrate in the purest sense. Many of the foods that are ultrahigh in carbohydrates are also fat-free or low in fat. So far, carbohydrates sound great.

But carbohydrates are tricky because your body doesn't actually start burning them as a primary source of energy until your effort level gets rather high. That's why élite or advanced runners advocate eating a high-carbo diet. At their level of training, carbohydrates are essential. But most of us mere mortals need to look more honestly at the amount of carbohydrates we consume and the amount we burn.

At high-effort levels, our bodies burn lots of calories from carbohydrates. But most of us don't push ourselves on a regular basis to the 3- to 4-hour high-intensity workouts that advanced athletes train at most of the time. We don't subject ourselves to the pain, torture and agony that they do. We don't routinely deplete our carbohydrate reserves. We think we need to stuff ourselves on potatoes, bagels and pasta because that's what we think athletes do.

However, while your body burns carbohydrates quickly, it can store only so many calories in your muscles in the form of glucose. Athletes have known this for a long time, which is why there is the traditional high-carbohydrate pre-race pasta party before so many marathons. Of course, those dinners were a part of the tradition long before we had sports drinks and energy gels, which do a much better job of providing carbos than fettuccini. But traditions are hard to break.

How much carbohydrate is just right for you? The balanced amount. Most of the time, you should gravitate toward quality, complex carbohydrates from whole grains, fruits and vegetables. No meal needs to be 100-per cent carbohydrate. In fact, every meal should contain some carbohydrates along with some protein and even some fat. Avoid empty carbohydrates from soft drinks, sweets and white bread unless you need a quick boost just before a run or race.

Allow yourself a moderate amount of fat. Fat – the stuff in cheeseburgers and cashews – has earned such a bad reputation that many runners literally race away from it. But just as many runners gorge on too much carbohydrate, they tend to cut too much fat from their diets. Again, balance is the key.

Your body needs fat for a number of processes. The most important ones for running are developing immunity and repairing muscle.

an exercise in joy

Just for a day, keep a diary of what you eat. Are your meals balanced with some healthy carbohydrate, protein, and fat sources? Or are they leaning heavily in one direction? Are you eating at least three meals a day?

Use what you learn to make some constructive changes in your eating plan. For example, you might vow to better balance your meals. Or you might strive to eat several small meals rather than two huge ones. The food choices you make will go a long way towards helping you feel energized during your runs.

When you don't eat enough fat, you're likely to catch colds more easily – which can remove the joy from running faster than you can say 'flu' and to suffer from more than your fair share of muscle soreness. Fat also serves another purpose: it takes a long time to break down in your gut, so it helps you to feel satisfied longer after a meal. A no-fat diet simply isn't the answer.

That doesn't mean you can go out and eat all of the cheeseburgers and chips you want. After all, fat always has been and still is fattening. Plus, some types of fat, such as the saturated fats in animal products and the trans fats in processed foods, have been linked to heart disease and cancer.

What's the answer? Allow yourself a small amount of healthy fat with every meal. Healthy fats can be found in olive oil, avocados, nuts, peanut butter, fatty fish and olives.

Don't forget about protein. And what about protein? Your body uses protein as the principal source for rebuilding muscle. If you're exercising to the point of breaking down muscle tissue (which occurs when you raise the effort level past 50 per cent of maximum), you need protein. You get protein from meat, dairy, and nuts as well as from protein drinks. Try to eat a healthy, low-saturated fat protein source with every meal, such as skimmed milk or non-fat yoghurt at breakfast, tofu at lunch and chicken or fish at dinner.

Feast or Famine

So what can you do? You can start by eating like a normal human being. You continue by learning to adjust the mix of what you're eating based on what you're doing. As long as you don't get carried away with any particular point of view, it's not hard to eat the way your body wants you to eat.

If you're hungry all the time, you aren't eating enough. Or, at the very least, you're eating food that your body is burning so fast that it's demanding you replenish it. If you're increasing your activity but still have to buy larger-size clothes, then you're eating foods that your body is storing for later.

How much later, no one knows. Your body believes that when you starve it, there's no food available. Your body doesn't believe that you would intentionally deprive it of nourishment if nourishment were available. Would you? Would you *not* eat when there was food? Your body thinks you're smarter than that. If you're not putting food in your body, it believes that there's nothing for you to eat so it immediately slows down your metabolism, clings desperately to every ounce of fat that it can, and does its level best to keep you from starving to death.

lessons learned

Don't get hung up on your family and friends not understanding or being supportive of your running. Do it for yourself, or you spend a lot of emotional energy on this!

**– Kelly Ambrose, aged 43
Running for 6 years**

I wish I were as smart as my body thinks I am. At times when my refrigerator was full of food, I lived like I was in the midst of a world-wide famine. I knew I was getting sluggish, that I didn't feel like doing very much, that my body craved nourishment. But I continued to pretend there was nothing I could do.

On the other hand, if you feed and nourish your body on a regular basis, three or four times a day, it thinks you're living in times of great abundance. It believes you've arrived at the harvest and food will be plentiful. When that happens, your body begins to let go of the stored fat because it doesn't believe you'll need it. It starts to process the food you've eaten as a source of energy because it believes there will be more where that came from.

It's really no more complicated than that. It's a matter of learning to work with your body's natural impulses rather than against them. If you spend only a few minutes contemplating the beauty of the system already in place in your body, you'll throw every diet book you've ever bought out of the window.

I began to make better choices when I began to understand that my body had to process the food I put into it, turning that food from something I liked into something my body needed. I finally realized that my digestive system wasn't designed to convert hot-fudge sundaes into food that my body could use for anything other than storing fat around my waist.

I saw the relationship between my body and food as one that was more powerful than anything I could ever overcome. When that all clicked, when I started to view my digestive system as one of the components of an overall programme of fitness, the battle I had been fighting since my teenage years was over.

Dancing
with the Devil

Listen to your body and eliminate the four-letter word 'pain' from your running vocabulary

They tell a story about Bill Rodgers, the four-time winner of the Boston and New York marathons and now a regular on the dinner speaker circuit. When someone says they've met him at a previous event, he asks, 'How's the injury?' The shocked fan can't believe Bill remembered and launches into a description of the recovery, surgery or continuing problem. Of course, Bill doesn't remember. He's just smart enough to know that if a runner talked to him before, chances are he talked about his injury.

Such is the nature of runners. For all the rhetoric about learning to live a healthier, more active lifestyle, many new runners simply transfer their previous obsessive drive to this new area of their lives. Bill's experience, and mine, shows that there are only two kinds of adult athletes: those who have injured themselves by doing too much and those who are going to injure themselves by doing too much.

It seems inevitable that we take everything to the extreme. I know I did. Perhaps this phenomenon is peculiar to mature athletes. For some reason, we think there is honour in pushing our bodies past the point of fatigue and to the brink of injury. We take pride in the aches and pains that prove we've been working out. Many of us brag about how much pain we can take, as if the ability to push past our body's breaking point means more than that we are just stubborn.

I don't know what it's like for women, but young boys growing up in the shadow of World War II in the early 1950s played a lot of 'war'. In those days, playing war didn't mean standing in front of a video screen. It meant actually getting outside, shooting at each other with toy rifles and throwing mud grenades.

It was a matter of honour to get 'hit' and keep going. We spent hours grabbing our chests, flailing away on the ground like a fish on land, and then bouncing back into the battle. Being wounded wasn't something to be avoided. It was something to be sought.

It's no wonder that when I started to become more active, to walk and run further every day, I mistook the first onset of injury as a sign that I was doing all the right things. When I had to grab the handrail to climb the steps, I viewed it not as an overuse injury, but as my first athletic wound. I took pride in it!

As I entered more races, I discovered that having a running injury was like having a membership card into the club. I remember a local 5-K, the first event at which I had an obvious running injury. As I pulled on my knee brace, I actually got a little excited. Now I would have something to talk about with the real runners.

I'm not the only one. Stand in the middle of the pack at any local distance race. You'll think you've been transported to an orthopaedic conference. You'll see knee and ankle braces and enough elastic bandages to wrap Big Ben. No one seems the least bit concerned. It's accepted as part of the runner's way of life.

I was once asked how much of an anti-inflammatory one should take *during* a marathon. It seems that the inquirer had a knee problem and was concerned about being able to finish the race. I looked him right in the eye and told him that if the pain was so bad that he needed to medicate himself, he needed to *stop*!

Our culture doesn't help. Professional athletes who 'play through the pain' are revered. Those who can 'take a licking and keep on

ticking' are our heroes. I'm waiting for the day when the football com-
mentator says, 'Yes, Bob, his arm was torn off during that last charge,
but he's stuffed it into his jersey and is staying on the pitch. What a
man!' It's no wonder that many of us believe the path to true glory goes
through the physiotherapist's surgery.

The Quiet Voices of Your Body

It doesn't have to be that way. Learning to listen for the early warning
signs of overuse is one of the most important skills you can acquire. You
can learn to hear the whisper of your knees and the gentle sigh of your
hamstrings. You can learn to listen to the quiet voice of a body that
wants to get in better shape and stay in shape but doesn't want you to
work it so hard so soon that it breaks down.

As you start to become more active, you may experience fatigue,
soreness and a few new aches. But fatigue and soreness, even an ache,
are not the same as pain. Pain means injury is imminent or already
present.

lessons learned

*Before I started using a heart rate monitor (HRM), I would constantly push
myself. I'd also routinely pull my calf muscle every 8 or 10 months, resulting
in a 2- to 3-month layoff. Once I started using an HRM, I was forced to slow
down and haven't hurt my calf since. Sometimes on my last mile, it seems like
grandmas are passing me on their walking frames, but the numbers on the
HRM tell me that's OK. I'm getting better, even that slow.*

– Ken Johnson, aged 46
Running off and on for 4 years

Fatigue. When you move your leg through the running motion, you use various muscles such as the hamstrings, hip flexors and calf muscles. Muscles are funny. They don't work all the muscle fibres all the time. The muscles call for help when they need to, as they need to.

When you start moving a muscle, it uses as few fibres as possible to get the job done. As you fatigue the first fibres, others are recruited to do the work. The longer you keep moving the muscle, the more fibres are recruited until eventually, and in time, most of the muscle fibres are involved.

The fibres used earliest are the ones that are closest to being in shape already. They're the ones you use all the time anyway. When you start exercising, they're already fit enough to carry you without fatigue. But, if you've been inactive, there aren't very many fibres that are ready to go. The first fibres recruited almost immediately start calling for help from the fibres closest to them. Even though the second round of muscle fibres are near to the in-shape muscles, they're not as fit. The second-alarm muscles will tire much faster. When they do, they put out a third alarm.

The third level muscle isn't in as good shape as the second, so it tires even faster. And so on. As you work your muscles longer, more and deeper fibres are recruited from muscles that are weaker to begin with. When this happens, fatigue occurs almost immediately in those muscles furthest from the first level.

If you push too far through the fatigue, your body won't be able to support itself with muscle. Then, your joints and connecting tissues are recruited to do the work that the muscles should be doing. Because joints and tissue aren't designed to do this, injuries are right around the corner.

The bottom line is that you need to strengthen your muscles so they'll do what you want. As we've discussed, strength comes from stress *and* recovery. Muscles must be strengthened one level at a time, and adequate recovery time must be allowed at each level in order to get stronger.

Fatigue, the point at which the muscle starts to tire and has a more difficult time going through its range of motion, is good. You need to get to the point of fatigue. And then you need to stop. The fatigue point will change with time. Ultra runners, that rare breed who can run 50 to 100 miles or more, may never reach the point of fatigue. People like me may reach the point of fatigue 20 seconds into their first run.

Soreness. Soreness is fatigue that lasts a little longer. It lingers. Your legs may be tired and sore when you get out of bed or stand up after having been seated for a while. This is sometimes referred to as delayed-onset muscle soreness, which is the feeling in your muscles and joints a day or so after a workout.

In and of itself, soreness is not necessarily a bad sign. At one time or another, all of us do too much. We run too far or too hard and the next day we're sore. It's not a big deal, as long as we recognize the soreness as what it is: the first sign that we have overstressed our muscles.

Soreness is a sign that we've tired all the muscles we normally use and that our body has had to recruit some of the less well-conditioned muscles. Whether you've been running for decades or days, you'll feel some soreness when your body recruits the muscles that aren't well-conditioned. It's natural. Soreness may linger for a day or so, but it shouldn't last long. Your body should recover rather quickly from simple, first-stage overuse if you let it – and that's the key.

What should you do, then, if you run too far for your body on Sunday and wake up on Monday a little sore? The answer is easy: rest. Give your muscles a chance to recover. Many of us aren't willing to do this. We run on Monday with our strong, conditioned muscles already tired and our less well-conditioned muscles already sore. Several days later, still without rest, we're running with muscles even less well-conditioned and even less well-trained.

None of the joints in our knees, hips or feet are getting the support they need. The weaker muscles can't hold the knee steady, can't keep the kneecap tracking properly and can't keep the hips in alignment. In no time, pieces of your body are moving in directions that they were never intended to move. Joints are twisting in ways they were never designed to twist. And you're moving ever closer to a serious injury.

It's amazing that you can avoid all of this by simply taking time off so that those stronger, well-conditioned muscles have a chance to

an exercise *in* joy

Get more in touch with your body. On your next run, do regular body checks every 10 minutes or once a mile. Scan your body from head to toe. How does your head feel? Your neck? Your shoulders? Your back? Your legs? Your knees? Your feet? Notice when you begin to tire and if anything begins to feel sore. The more you do this exercise, the more you'll recognize the early warning signs of injury, thereby preventing it before it starts.

recover. One extra day of rest can mean the difference between training well for years and working through a nagging injury for months.

Aches. An ache is deeper than soreness. Fatigue and soreness are often associated with movement, but an ache can be present all the time, whether you're moving or not. An ache is a dull pain that's annoying, although not debilitating, and it is not to be ignored.

Aches are almost always related to something other than a single muscle. An ache occurs in a joint like the hip or knee, or in a cluster of muscles like the lower back. It often means that you didn't do too much all at once, but rather that you're doing a little too much all the time.

An ache can also be a sign that something is out of adjustment in the larger system of your body. If your lower back aches, for example, it may indicate that you're stronger on one side of your body than the other, perhaps that you're running a little sideways. An ache won't always respond to rest alone. If there's a mechanical problem, such as a leg length discrepancy or if you need orthotics (artificial supports), resting may make the ache go away for a while, but it will return as soon as you resume activity.

Pain. Pain is not fatigue. Pain is not soreness. Pain is not even an ache. Pain is when a part of your body hurts so badly that you have to change something in order to continue, or you have to stop altogether. Pain is not your friend. Pain is not nature's way of telling you that you are tough. Pain is not something to take pride in or to brag about. Pain means that something in your body has broken down so seriously that it can't continue.

Pain comes in two forms. It can be immediate, dramatic pain that comes from some kind of trauma. You know what traumatic pain feels and looks like if you've sprained an ankle or seen someone tear up a knee. It's sudden. It's shocking. It's impossible to ignore. Most runners don't face traumatic pain very often. It does happen, of course. You can fall, take a bad step or twist the wrong way.

Runners more often have the sort of pain that begins quietly, builds insidiously and continues to the point where it can no longer be ignored. It's that nagging little pain at the side of your knee. You start by rubbing it after your run. You take an anti-inflammatory. As you continue to ignore the pain, it becomes necessary to stretch before and after your runs, and to take the anti-inflammatories before and after. Later, you stretch and take the anti-inflammatories during your run as well. Eventually, you shop for some kind of device to wrap around your knee to make the pain go away. And you take anti-inflammatories around the clock.

This pattern was a part of my running life for years. I was an expert at ignoring, then masking, pain so that I could keep running. When over-

lessons learned

I wish I'd known that when you run, especially when you are learning to run, you need to walk sometimes! I felt that to be a runner you had to run all the time until you were so exhausted that you couldn't move and could only barely breathe! Now, it's intervals. Some days 4:1 and some days 5:1. Eventually, I'll get to 10:1 or maybe not have to walk at all. But for now, I cut 8 minutes off my 5-K PR (personal record) the first time I included some walking (4:1).

– Myles Drynan, aged 38
Running for 1 year

the-counter anti-inflammatories stopped working, I switched to prescrip-
tion-strength medication. I increased the dosage of one particular NSAID
(nonsteroidal anti-inflammatory drug) to which I had an allergy until my
lips were swollen. It wasn't pretty. Then I knew I was at my limit!

It took me a long time to learn that there is no such thing as pain
management, except for very short periods of time. If being active is
something you want to do for the rest of your life, you need to take a
much longer-term view.

We all dance with the devil now and then. No one who has been a
runner for any length of time will tell you honestly that they've never
run with soreness, an ache, or even with pain. But they will tell you that
they knew they were taking a calculated risk and that it's not something
they did on a regular basis.

Learning to respect your body is an important step in becoming an
athlete. Learning to work with your body and learning to allow it to get
stronger on its own terms is as essential to your success as running itself.
Becoming a partner with your body in achieving your goals is the only
strategy that will ever work.

You must learn that there will be days when the best training you
can do is no training. You must learn that it takes no discipline at all to
ignore the subtle signs of overuse and go on with your training programme. The real discipline is doing not what is necessary for your ego
but what you know is right for your body.

It takes more courage to rest an extra day or to put an extra '0' in
your training log than it does to limp through a workout. It takes more
discipline to stop running when you first feel pain than to 'gut it out'
and finish the run.

You'll know you're a runner when you understand that the body
you have is the only one you're going to get, that you don't get to
exchange it for a new one if you break it. You'll know you're a runner
when you begin making decisions about when to run based on the col-
laboration between your mind and your body.

Avoiding the dance with the devil comes down to a simple rule:
don't do anything today that might keep you from running tomorrow.

Basic Truths about

Injury Prevention

Everything you need to know to prevent injuries
and to run ache- and pain-free

There's an old saying among motorcyclists that also applies to runners: 'There are only two kinds of riders: those who have been down and those who are going to go down.' It isn't that motorcyclists are cynical; they just recognize the inherent risks of riding. Sometimes I think runners should be as intelligent!

Another motorcycling adage bears on a discussion of injuries: 'There are old riders and bold riders, but there are no old, bold riders.' In other words, if you continue to take unnecessary risks, you will run out of luck at some point.

As runners, we are faced with a dilemma: how can you maximize your training and minimize your risk of injury? It's not only the new runner who must answer this question. Runners of all ages and experience levels must be aware of their bodies' ever changing tolerance of the stresses of training. Even the most astute, aware athlete sometimes steps over the line of good sense. Perhaps a run is going so well that you ignore that niggling little pain. A race-day PR (personal record, or your best time at a certain distance) seems possible if you just push past that little ache. It happens to all of us, but when it does, injury is inevitable.

Running is generally a safe fitness pursuit. Unlike cyclists, few runners take a fall hard enough to cause a concussion or break a collarbone, and unlike swimmers, runners simply can't drown. That said, runners do tend to get injured or hurt in predictable places for predictable reasons. The good news is that nearly all aches and pains can be prevented.

Signs, Causes and Prevention

A few runners get hurt dramatically – by twisting an ankle, tripping over a root or falling and breaking a bone. But most runners experience pain much more slowly over a period of time by overusing and abusing their bodies.

The vast percentage of running injuries are caused by overuse. It's not that runners are more foolish than the rest of the population; it's that, once we're hooked on it, we hate the idea of *not* running. Many of us, especially those who started running later in life, continue to press on in the face of injury because we don't want to stop having fun.

Runners talk about injuries as if it's impossible to work out why or how they occur. It's no mystery! Most injuries are avoidable because we bring them on ourselves: we run too many miles; we run too fast; we run too often too soon; we run too hard on our easy days; we keep running in old shoes that have lost their effectiveness; we run when we know we're too tired. The bottom line is that we control our own destinies. We just aren't very good at it.

Preventing overuse injuries before they start is your best defence against pain. Your best tactic, again, is learning to listen to the subtle signals your body sends your way. Most overuse injuries develop in stages.

Stage 1: Grumpiness. One of the first signs of an impending overuse injury (or that you're doing too much too soon) shows up in your attitude, not in your body. If you find that you're waking up 'cranky' or if you're chronically impatient with those around you for no apparent reason, it's very likely that you need a few days off. Your body is sending a signal to your head that it needs a break.

Stage 2: The sniffles. If you find yourself coming down with colds or the flu more often than usual, if you have trouble falling asleep or aren't sleeping soundly, if you seem to get out of breath easily, or if you have more aches and pains than normal, you're probably on the edge of being overtrained. When that happens, there's only one thing to do: rest!

Stage 3: Ouch. This is the stage when most of us actually take notice. Generally, we tend to blame our bodies. 'Why is my knee acting up now?!' we ask incredulously. If we had listened to our bodies during the first two stages, stage three never would have occurred.

Besides taking the rest your body needs, you can also avoid common aches and pains by making sure your body is 'balanced'. Running typically strengthens and tightens the same predictable muscles. Most runners have tight calves and hamstrings, while their shins and inner and outer thighs are weak.

If you add the following injury-proofing moves to your programme two to three times a week after your runs, you will be able to prevent most injuries from popping up.

Stretch. So simple, yet so ignored. Focus on the muscles that tend to get tight: the calves and hamstrings. If you have time, your hips and quadriceps could use some stretching as well. Try to stretch after your runs, when your muscles are warm.

Do leg lifts. Those old-fashioned Jane Fonda leg lifts are just what you need. Strap on a pair of ankle weights, lie on your side and lift your top leg straight up and down until your outer thigh feels tired. Then do the same with your bottom leg. Then flip over and do the same on your other side. Do this routine three times a week.

Cross-train. You'll learn more about this in 'Basic Truths about Cross-Training' on page 148. Anything you can do to complement running – from cycling to swimming to rock climbing – will help you develop well-rounded strength and flexibility.

Wear good shoes. The best shoes for you are the ones that complement your foot type. Very often, when runners start to feel an ache, simply switching to a different type of shoe will solve the problem.

Overuse injuries that affect runners result from repeated stress over a long period of time. Deciding when to stop running can be difficult, because in many cases, especially in the early stages, pain from the injury isn't severe enough to keep us from running. In fact, some kinds of injuries actually feel better for a while when we run. My rules for assessing the likelihood and severity of an overuse injury are simple.

- If the pain persists for more than 5 minutes after you begin your run, *stop*.
- If the pain forces you to alter your running gait, *stop*.
- If the pain persists for *less* than 30 minutes after a run, take the next day off.
- If the pain persists for *more* than 30 minutes after a run, take the next 3 days off.

Resting doesn't always mean stopping completely. It may just mean reducing your mileage and intensity for a week or so. For example, you might omit your long run and speedwork for a couple weeks. If the pain persists for more than two weeks despite all the other precautions you've taken, seek professional help.

RICE-ing Your Injury

So, you ignored all the warning signs, neglected your stretching, and now something hurts. You can still nip this early on, before it gets so bad that you must take multiple weeks off the roads. The first course of self-treatment for virtually all running injuries is RICE therapy: Rest, Ice, Compression and Elevation. RICE will help reduce pain, inflammation and swelling from overuse injuries, as well as acute ones like sprains, strains and bruises.

Rest. Rest means avoiding any kind of activity that aggravates the injury, provokes the pain or risks making the injury worse. There's wisdom in the old joke about the patient who complains, 'Doctor, what should I do? My arm hurts when I do this.' The doctor replies, 'Then don't do that!' Rest means avoiding *all* activities, not just running, that might affect or irritate the injured area.

This means you should *not* constantly 'test' the area to see if it still hurts. I doubt that I'm the only person alive who does this. It's natural to keep touching a toothache to see if it still hurts. If your knee aches when you step a certain way, your tendency is to step that way several times a day to confirm your diagnosis – or in hopes that the ache will have magically disappeared.

Ice. Treat the injured area with an ice pack as soon as possible, ideally within the first 5 to 10 minutes, to help reduce the swelling and inflammation. Keep the ice pack in place for about 20 minutes, then reapply it once every 2 hours for the next 48 hours. Put a damp towel between your skin and the ice pack to prevent freezing your skin.

The most inexpensive yet effective 'mouldable' ice pack is a package of frozen peas. You'll be surprised at how well a 450 g (1 lb) package of frozen peas conforms to most of the body parts you're likely to injure. Another inexpensive ice device can be made by freezing water, with an ice lolly stick in it, in a small paper cup. Remove the lolly from the cup and massage the injured area for 15 to 20 minutes.

Compression. Compression also reduces swelling. Use firm but gentle pressure – this is not the time to torture yourself! You can apply compression when you're icing and when you're not. Wrap the area with compression tape or an elastic bandage except when you're sleeping. This will discourage swelling. When you're icing the injury, apply compression by taping or bandaging the ice pack on the affected area. (Be careful not to get the ice pack so tight that you cut off your circulation, and remember to put a damp towel between your skin and the ice pack.)

Elevation. If possible, elevate the injured area, keeping it above your heart. Lie on the floor and prop your foot up against the wall, or lie on the bed or sofa, using pillows to raise your foot or leg above your heart. This reduces the effect of gravity, preventing blood and fluid from pooling around the injury, reducing the swelling and inflammation.

How to Treat the Most Common Running Injuries

Nothing will remove the joy from running faster than an injury. In fact, nothing is as likely to prevent you from running altogether! When you get injured, don't get neurotic about your lack of smart training. First, your body alignment may simply predispose you to particular aches and pains. Second, we all get injured. It seems to be built into our running psyche.

But you don't have to stay injured. Here's a guide to some of the most common injuries and treatments to help you get back on your feet as soon as possible.

Iliotibial Band Syndrome

The IT band is the large ligament that extends from the outside of your pelvis and attaches just below the outside of your knee. Iliotibial Band

Syndrome, what runners call IT Band Syndrome, is one of the most common running complaints. Sooner or later, almost every runner has some kind of pain on the outside of their knee, especially in the early stages of running.

The IT band moves back and forth across your thigh bone and helps to stabilize the knee. Repeated rubbing of the band over the knee bone and repetitive bending and straightening of the knee while you run can cause the band to become irritated or the whole area to become inflamed. This can result in an isolated stinging or 'pin-prick' type pain on the outside of your leg just above or below the knee, or you may feel a dull pain along the whole length of the IT band.

As you continue to run, IT band pain gradually gets worse. The pain occurs when your foot strikes the ground and persists after you stop running. It can be particularly painful when running downhill or walking down stairs. The pain can also be caused by increasing your distance too quickly, by biomechanical problems such as bowed legs or overpronation, or by running on a cambered surface (e.g., always running against traffic on the same side of a road that curves up towards the centre). Because of the greater angle between their hips and knees, women are especially susceptible to IT band pain.

lessons learned

My first two pairs of shoes gave me terrible blisters, but I thought that was just part of running, so I lived with it. By accident I found my third pair, which were wonderful – not one blister! Before that, I honestly thought that blisters were part of breaking in new shoes, and you just had to deal with them until your feet toughened up. (This means I also wish I knew about wicking socks; I wore cotton up until a couple of months ago, which I'm sure didn't help with the blistering!)

– Nancy Volkers, aged 33
Running for 3 years

If you have pain in the IT band, the first thing to do is to ice the area and take a few days off to reduce the inflammation. You then need to adjust your training routine by reducing your mileage during the next several weeks.

Use this time to evaluate both your training schedule and your training surfaces. Ask the questions that will help you to avoid the injury in the future. Did you increase your mileage too quickly? Are you running the same direction on a track all the time? Are the streets you run on cambered? Are you wearing running shoes that correct any biomechanical problems?

Effective long-term treatment really comes down to not over-doing it at any point. Many experts will encourage you to stretch the IT band as well, but my experience is that stretching an inflamed IT band is very likely to prolong irritation and recovery. Once the area is healed and you are no longer experiencing pain, gentle post-run stretching and/or a programme to strengthen your thigh and hip muscles may help.

Plantar Fasciitis

The plantar fascia is a tendon-like band of tissue that runs along the bottom of the foot, between the heel bone and the base of the toes. Plantar fasciitis, what runners call PF, is the chronic pain through your foot's arch area. The most common site of the pain is on the bottom of the heel.

The running motion causes the plantar fascia to stretch and pull, which can lead to irritation and inflammation. The most dramatic symptom of PF is a noticeable pain with the first few steps you take after getting out of bed in the morning. The plantar fascia contracts at night, so when you put weight on your foot and stretch the fascia the first time in the morning, the pain may be severe.

Runners ignore PF because the pain usually subsides as you move around during the day. This is especially misleading because the pain may disappear while you run. Activity causes the plantar fascia to loosen up, and there is less or no pain. But that doesn't mean the problem is gone.

Runners with a high arch or a rigid foot are susceptible to PF, as are people with flat feet who overpronate. Running in improper or worn out shoes that don't correct overpronation problems can cause PF. It can also be caused by shoes that are so rigid or stiff that they don't flex where your feet flex. You can test this easily by holding your shoe at the heel and toe and then bending it. If the shoe bends in the middle of the sole or not at all, it may be stressing your plantar fascia and causing it to stretch.

PF may also result from running too much on your forefoot. Forefoot running works for sprinters who are only running a few hundred metres, but distance runners need to develop a running gait that brings the heel down first and distributes the stress of running along the entire foot.

Treating PF is tricky because there are so many possible causes. One of your first tasks will be to identify and eliminate all the factors that might have contributed to the problem. Do this one factor at a time, beginning with the most obvious ... like running in the same pair of shoes for three years. For short-term treatment, take a few days off, ice the area, and reduce the inflammation. If recommended by your

Inspirational
Tools of the Trade

Before you turn the page, make sure you've done everything you can to eliminate pain, burnout and staleness in your running. To ensure years of joyful perspiration, make sure you have:

1. Examined your nutritional programme, putting the focus on balanced meals.
2. Examined your shoes. Is it time to replace them? Are they the right size and shape for your foot type?
3. Examined your training habits. Are you taking enough rest, doing enough stretching and giving your body the benefit of the doubt?

doctor, taking an anti-inflammatory medication such as aspirin or ibuprofen may help.

Long-term solutions include considering whether you need orthotics to correct overpronation problems that prevent the plantar fascia from fully extending. You may have very good luck with an over-the-counter orthotic, such as the brands Spenco or Superfeet. In more severe cases, you may need a prescription orthotic from a chiropodist.

Again, as with the IT band, stretching while the pain is present is not a strategy that I recommend. When the pain is gone, a stretching routine to increase the flexibility of your feet and calf muscles may help prevent PF from recurring.

Achilles Tendinitis

The Achilles tendon attaches to the back of the heel and extends up the rear of the leg. It can be a very difficult injury to treat if it is not addressed early. Achilles tendinitis occurs when the tendon is inflamed or, in severe cases, ruptures. The first symptoms are likely to be a burning pain above the heel bone or a shooting pain that occurs during activity, especially on hills or during speedwork. The area may become tender to the touch. If the tendon becomes so weak that it ruptures, it will cause a whole lot of pain.

The initial Achilles tendinitis pain can come from something as simple as the heel counter on your shoe being too high, causing the top of the heel portion of the shoe to rub against the Achilles tendon. The solution is easy: get a different pair of shoes.

Other causes of Achilles tendinitis are overpronation, supination, high arches, increasing your mileage or intensity too much or too soon (Are you beginning to see a pattern here?), beginning your runs without properly warming up, or a programme of high mileage without adequate rest.

Short-term treatment is the same as for other overuse injuries. Take a few days off to let the inflammation subside. Consider anti-inflammatories if your doctor recommends them. Rub the heel area with ice after your runs. And, avoid running on hills.

For long-term treatment and to avoid recurrence, you'll need to address the causes of the Achilles tendinitis in the same way as you would plantar fasciitis. Look at your running routine, route and schedule, as well as at your shoes. You may need shoes with more heel cushioning or a small heel lift to reduce the strain on the Achilles tendon. An over-the-counter orthotic that raises the heel or prescription orthotics that correct your gait may be necessary.

Stress Fractures

Stress fractures are tiny breaks or cracks in the bones of the feet, legs, pelvis or hip area that are caused by repetitive trauma or overuse. While a stress fracture can occur at any time, they are usually caused by long periods of continued impact. Although you can get a stress fracture anywhere, the most common area for runners is in the foot.

Stress fractures are one of the most insidious running injuries because they begin so quietly that it's easy to ignore the symptoms. You might feel a little tenderness across the top of your foot, for example, but dismiss it as being caused by tying your shoes too tightly that day. Even when the pain intensifies and there is swelling in the area, the fracture generally progresses so gradually that we convince ourselves it's getting better if it doesn't hurt 'as much' as it used to. Even when we concede to the pain, an X-ray may not reveal the fracture.

Stress fractures are caused by increasing your mileage or intensity too quickly; returning to intense running too soon after a layoff; running too much on a hard running surface; or wearing a shoe that's not right for your foot, your running style or the surface on which you run. Running may not be the sole culprit, either. If you cross-train, be aware that other impact activities, such as dancing and aerobics, can cause stress fractures.

Stress fractures, even the *hint* of a stress fracture, are not to be taken lightly. Short-term treatment is immediate rest and immediate discontinuation of the activity. Icing and elevation are necessary. If the pain and swelling don't go away after a week of this treatment or if you begin to have difficulty with your normal, daily activities, get professional orthopaedic help.

Long-term treatment may require a cast to eliminate further stress if the fracture is in the lower leg or the foot, or a heel cup to protect the area if the fracture is in the heel. You may have to use crutches to get the weight and pressure off your foot or leg. The doctor may also prescribe medication to reduce the swelling. Depending on the location and severity of the injury, a stress fracture can take from 4 to 26 weeks to heal. (No, that's not a typo: 26 weeks. Six months!) Even though the pain may go away within the first few weeks, the risk of re-injury is so great that you must give the fracture plenty of time to fully heal.

Chondromalacia Patellae

Almost 25 per cent of all injuries treated in sports clinics are for chondromalacia patellae, what runners call runner's knee. Anyone can have it, and if they're not careful, almost everyone will.

Runner's knee is the inflammation and softening of the cartilage under the kneecap. When the cartilage becomes inflamed, the kneecap (or patella) doesn't slide up and down smoothly. The pain and swelling associated with runner's knee appear gradually. Over time (sometimes as much as a year), you'll typically feel the pain underneath or on both sides of the kneecap. The pain intensifies during sports activities, when going down stairs or hills, and after sitting with the knee bent for extended periods of time. You may also have a crackling feeling that you can actually hear in the knee.

Runner's knee results from poor conditioning or muscle imbalances. Weak quadriceps muscles that don't hold the patella in place, overpronation and running on a highly crowned road can cause it. If it isn't addressed soon or thoroughly enough, runner's knee can easily become a chronic problem.

To treat runner's knee, take a few days off to allow the inflammation to subside, reduce your training volume, ice the area and consider anti-inflammatories, if recommended by your doctor. Long-term rehabilitation should include a strength-training programme to balance your leg muscles side-to-side and front-to-back. If you eliminate the causes, runner's knee will not prevent you from continuing to run.

Shinsplints

Small tears in the leg muscles where they attach to the shin cause shinsplints. The pain starts as a dull ache on the inside of the shin, especially in the bottom half of the leg, during or after running. The first dull pain may be followed by tenderness and swelling, with the pain increasing until even walking is difficult.

Wearing wrong or worn out shoes can contribute to getting shinsplints. Increasing your mileage or intensity can also cause them. (Surprise, surprise!) By now I hope you've realized that *nothing* good ever comes from increasing your mileage or intensity too quickly.

Like other running injuries, the short-term treatment for shinsplints is to take a few days off so that the inflammation subsides, ice, reduce your mileage and intensity for a few weeks, and avoid hills. You should *never* try to run through the pain of shinsplints. Long-term rehabilitation should include a strength-training programme to help reduce the muscle imbalances that contribute to shinsplints.

lessons learned

Here's the one thing I wish I had known before I laced up the old running shoes: build the base before you do the race, and put in the time before you toe the line. Translated, it means that marathons are not the end all, be all of running. It makes absolutely no sense to run a marathon during your first year of running. The only thing important during your first year is building your base – doing all those things that strengthen the muscles, tendons, etc., which allow you to grow as a runner with minimal risk of injury. In essence, become a runner before you become a racer and then, if you so desire, the Mt Everest of running will be easier to climb.

– Phillip Oppenheim, aged 57
Running for 10 years

Other Nuisances

The following list of pains and maladies are not necessarily injury related. But, like injuries, they can remove the joy from running if you don't learn how to circumvent them.

Sciatica. Sciatica is, literally, a pain in the buttock. The pain produced often either radiates from the buttocks down the back or side of your leg, or over and around it. You may mistake sciatica for a hamstring problem.

Sciatic pain doesn't necessarily come while you're running. It may bother you while you're sitting – in the car, watching television or working at your desk. It can be very difficult to diagnose and may lead you to seek the counsel of witch doctors and a cosmic medium in search of a cure.

If it sounds like I know something about sciatic pain, I *do*. I chased around a pain in the rear for nearly two years. I stopped biking, stopped running for a while, lifted weights, stretched, and had an X-ray, an MRI and a bone scan. I took cortisone injections in the upper and lower hip. I changed shoes, socks, running routes and religions. Nothing helped.

Then I got a new office chair and the pain magically disappeared. My office chair had kept me in a position that pinched the nerve. With the new chair, I had *no* pain. I still have to be careful about certain sitting positions, especially in cars and on aeroplanes, but sciatica has never bothered my running again.

If a new chair doesn't solve the problem for you, the usual means of self-treatment apply: anti-inflammatories if recommended by your doctor, very gentle stretching of the hamstrings and lower back muscles, and, of course, rest and reduction in your running mileage.

Side stitches. Most runners consider side stitches to be a nuisance, not an injury, but if you've experienced severe side stitches, you know they can be more than annoying during a race or run. There are as many theories about the causes and cures of side stitches as people who suffer from them.

Side stitches appear to have something to do with the functioning of the diaphragm. Runners speculate that the diaphragm may have a cramp or spasm; that an organ may be pulling down on the diaphragm; or that it may be caused by eating too soon before you run, drinking too much water before you run, or from breathing too shallowly. The truth is that no one knows for sure.

Slowing down seems to be the best first line of defence. If you slow down or stop and get your breathing regulated, the stitch will often go away. Changing the foot on which you exhale may help. If you're breathing out when your right foot strikes, try breathing out when the left foot strikes. Another strategy is to raise your hands over your head while you run. It may not always make the pain go away, but it will entertain the runners around you.

Blisters. Blisters are the bane of many runners' existence, while others run for years without experiencing this troublesome and painful affliction. Blisters are caused when something rubs against a patch of skin. The resulting heat causes the body to protect itself by creating a liquid barrier of blood, pus or fluid. The best way to cure a blister is to do all you can to prevent it.

Some runners go to extreme lengths to protect themselves against blisters. A good friend of mine, an ultra runner of many years, rubs petroleum jelly over his feet, dons a pair of women's knee-high nylons, and *then* puts on his running socks and shoes.

Eliminating cotton socks from your running wardrobe is the first step in avoiding blisters. Cotton soaks up sweat, gets wet and lumpy, and then bad things start to happen. A good pair of CoolMax socks may help you avoid blisters. Double-layer CoolMax socks work for some runners, although my personal experience suggests that they aren't very effective in wet running conditions. The extra padding of heavier socks is designed to protect sensitive areas of the feet that are especially prone to friction.

Covering your feet with Vaseline, Body Glide or some other friction-reducing salve or ointment may work for some runners, but it can also cause the foot to slide more easily and blister more quickly. Protective pads are available to protect sensitive parts of the feet. Some adhesive plaster manufacturers make rubbery adhesive pads that can be wrapped around or placed over areas that are blister prone. These products can be a godsend to those who suffer from chronic blisters.

Sooner or later most of us will have one of those nasty bubbles somewhere on our feet. There are two schools of thought on treatment: pop them or leave them alone. Which you choose comes down to the strength of your convictions and the strength of your stomach.

If you're a popper, be sure to thoroughly sterilize the needle before you pierce the blister. Boiling water is best, but a flame will do in a pinch. After breaking the blister, drain out as much of the fluid as possible, then apply a pressure pad for several days. Or, if the blister isn't driving you crazy, you can let nature take its course. Most blisters will cure themselves in a few days. The potential danger is that blisters can become infected. In that case, you should see a doctor for treatment.

Black toenails. Never go swimming with a group of marathon runners. You'll see some of the nastiest, ugliest, most disgusting toes you've ever come across. If you're dating a marathon runner, be sure to ask them to remove their socks *before* you commit to marriage.

Black toenails, and the loss of toenails, are almost always the result of wearing shoes that are too small. It may be ego or ignorance, but a runner who is forever walking around with black toenails or spends half his running life waiting for toenails to fall off, is missing the point.

Your feet swell when you run. They swell a *lot* when you run for a long time in hot weather. A shoe that feels right at the beginning of a long run may be a size too small two hours later. When buying shoes, be sure that there is *at least* a thumb's width between your *longest* toe and the end of your running shoe. The repeated impact to the front of your toes from shoes that are too short causes blood to pool under the toenail.

In addition, a shoe that fits with a thin pair of socks can be too small with a thicker pair. When you shop for running shoes, go late in the day and bring the socks you plan to wear with those shoes. I often shop for running shoes in the afternoon after I've done a long run in the morning. My feet are as swollen then as they're ever going to be and I end up with shoes that fit well for my long runs.

Coming Back from an Injury

We often joke that the middle of the pack at almost any local race looks like a medical convention. You'll see runners with almost every body part taped, wrapped and braced. It would be funny if it weren't so sad. The goal is to run forever, not just this weekend. Coming back from a running injury is immensely frustrating, but the patience and discipline you show during your recovery will be worth it. Take your time.

In a later chapter we will talk about cross-training activities. Sports like bicycling and swimming can be great cardiovascular workouts, as well as excellent ways to stay fit while recovering from an injury. Water or pool running can keep you in shape while you heal so that you needn't start from scratch when you come back.

No one wants to have an injury, but they can and do happen. How you react to them will play a big part in your career as a runner. There are times when being the best runner you can be means not running at all.

Recommended Reading

▶ Anderson, Bob. *Stretching*. 20th anniversary edition. Bolinas, CA: Shelter Publications, 2000.

▶ Applegate, Liz. *Power Foods: High-Performance Nutrition for High-Performance People*. Emmaus, PA: Rodale Inc., 1994.

▶ Clark, Nancy. *Nancy Clark's Sports Nutrition Guidebook*. 2nd edition. Champaign, IL: Human Kinetics, 1996.

▶ Ellis, Joe and Joe Henderson. *Running Injury-Free: How to Prevent, Treat and Recover from Dozens of Painful Problems*. Emmaus, PA: Rodale Inc., 1994.

▶ Feldman, Andrew. *The Jock Doc's Body Repair Kit: The New Sports Medicine for Recovery and Increased Performance*. New York, NY: St. Martin's Press, 2000.

► Micheli, Lyle J. and Mark Jenkins. *Healthy Runner's Handbook.* Champaign, IL: Human Kinetics, 1996.

► Micheli, Lyle J. and Mark Jenkins. *The Sports Medicine Bible: Prevent, Detect, and Treat Your Sports Injuries Through the Latest Medical Techniques.* New York, NY: HarperCollins, 1995.

Part 3
Dedication

Staying the Course

The key to running for the rest of your life is not discipline – it's dedication!

Those who know me well know that I enjoy participating in marathons. I'm careful to say 'participating' because I've never actually *run* a marathon (I use a run/walk method for long distances), let alone raced one. Still, for me, the act of standing at a start line 26.2 miles from a finish line is the purest metaphor for living an active life. If I keep moving forwards, if I keep putting one foot in front of the other – in the marathon and in my life – I will see myself through to the end.

It hasn't always been that way. For much of my life, I only believed in what I couldn't do. I tried something, did it well enough to enjoy it, tried to get better, became frustrated by my inability, and then gave up. The same is true for others, which is why I don't trust the power of inspiration in and of itself. Being inspired is fine for a week or two, and being motivated might work for a month or so. But to make any lifestyle change last a lifetime, you need dedication.

Dedication sometimes means doing what you don't want to do. I hear people talk about discipline. Some think that I'm a very disciplined person because I lost so much weight and have trained for so many marathons. Nonsense. I think I'm about the least disciplined person I've ever known. I've always had an irrepressible spirit that doesn't respond well to discipline. A rigid environment is like a prison to me. Discipline is not my strong suit. But I'd go so far as to suggest that many of the élite runners I've met aren't disciplined either.

What élite runners are, what I think I am, and what I am encouraging you to be is dedicated, not disciplined. I want you to be dedicated to a life of activity – to making better choices about food and to making the most out of whatever physical talents and skills you possess.

Most of what I've learned about dedication comes from my career as a musician and music teacher. I began playing the trombone when I was eight years old, with no more talent for the trombone than anything else, but my mother had played the instrument, still had her old one in the attic, and lessons were free. That's all it took to turn me into a trombone player.

For the next 30 years I defined myself by the sounds that came from my instrument. I made my friends and my livelihood with the trombone and *only* with the trombone. There was no contact with the outside world for me. My view of the world was always over the bell of the horn.

lessons learned

I wish I knew it was 'OK' to walk, and that walking didn't somehow negate the distance I ran. When I first started running, I would run until exhaustion, then stop the workout. This made for many depressing weeks during which I ran only a mile or even less than a mile, finishing tired and discouraged. It was only when I started training for my first marathon that I learned about walk breaks. I imagine my first 6 months of running would have been much more pleasant if I'd known about them back then, too!

– Nancy Volkers, aged 33
Running for 3 years

There's something to be said, I suppose, for those of us who create our very lives by making music with twisted pieces of brass or hollowed-out pieces of wood. We've accepted certain challenges and risks. Musicians, artists and athletes are not very different in that sense.

Throughout my performing career, I searched for the magic plan that would change me from a merely excellent craftsman into a truly exceptional artist. Working so hard to find the magic wasn't the result of discipline; it was the result of dedication. I was dedicated to finding the secret that would reveal the mysteries of the instrument, to finding the answer that I knew all trombonists were looking for.

During those 30 years of practising scales and arpeggios, playing the same technical exercise for the 1,000th time, and putting my lips against the mouthpiece over and over, I never discovered the secret. But I learned that you can never tell how close you are to real improvement and you can never be sure what's just ahead. Improvement for me as a musician always appeared unannounced.

Dedication versus Discipline

It's been the same for me as a runner, except that the little talent I had as a musician was far more than I have as a runner. Still, the mystery about when and where improvement will come is exactly the same. Very often there's no hint that a breakthrough is a single run away. That's why dedication is so much more important than discipline. It isn't the run that you do or don't do that counts. It isn't the discipline to run three days a week that makes you a runner. It's the dedication to run for the rest of your life that matters.

Part of my dedication comes from wanting to find the answers to a few simple questions. For example, no one has been able to explain to my satisfaction why running at a certain pace is easy one day and impossible the next. No one has explained to my satisfaction why I can run a marathon with apparent ease and later struggle to get through a

3-mile run. Despite all the research and opinions, I've decided that no one really knows.

Doctors, coaches and sports physiologists explain that it has something to do with muscle fatigue and dehydration. They tell you about the effects of stress and lack of sleep. They describe how nutrition and blood sugar levels affect performance. But the truth is that no one knows.

I don't either, but I'm dedicated to finding an answer. It's one reason I continue to put on my running shoes. If I thought I could find the answer another way, I might try, but I'm sure that it's only by running today, tomorrow and the rest of my life that I'm going to find the answer. Every day I run I feel like I'm a little closer to unlocking the secret.

What that means to me is that no single run is any more important than any other run. Being dedicated to finding the secret means that a difficult run, or one that takes every bit of enthusiasm I can muster to finish, is no better than the run when I feel like I'm floating on air. I might enjoy the latter more than the former, but I understand the importance of both. Being a dedicated rather than a disciplined runner means understanding that frustration is an important part of the combination of ingredients that leads to progress. For the dedicated runner, frustration is to be sought out and savoured, not avoided.

I learned this as a musician, too. When I heard other trombonists practising, I often thought that they played much better than I did. I heard them playing a solo or étude and wondered how I could ever be that good. Hearing them caused me to doubt my own talent and desire.

I practised differently than most of them. When I practised, I sounded terrible. My practice technique was to concentrate on the aspects of my playing that weren't any good. I spent hours, weeks, even years trying to learn how to do what I couldn't do. I finally realized that what I heard in other practice rooms was people playing what they already knew how to play. Their egos wouldn't allow them to sound bad or to try something new. They were avoiding frustration.

Frustration Is Good for You

Frustration is the first step towards improvement. I have no incentive to improve if I'm content with what I can do and if I'm completely satisfied with my pace, distance and form as a runner. It's only when I face frustration and use it to fuel my dedication that I feel myself moving forwards.

It's equally important to understand that where you start isn't nearly as important as the direction you're heading. If, like me, you're overweight and out of shape when you begin a life of activity, you have much more room for improvement.

Knowing that a breakthrough is always possible can give your daily runs the character of a treasure hunt. Stepping out the door or onto the treadmill, you can allow yourself to wonder if today is the day. You can allow yourself to look for, listen for and feel the small improvements that occur so often in the first few months of running.

You can allow yourself to accept your body's invitation to discover the treasure in that day's run. Not every run will reveal the Ark of the

lessons learned

I wish that I hadn't waited so long to start running with other people. I ran by myself for the first six months because I thought that I wouldn't be able to keep up with 'real' runners. When I started training with a group at the beginning of March (I'm preparing for my first half-marathon), everything got easier. I could keep up; I did fit in. The long runs are much more pleasant, the short ones are downright fun. I've made some friends, and – most importantly of all – I've learned first-hand that all one has to do to be a 'real' runner is run. We're all real runners.

– Jennifer Dupas, aged 29
Running for 2 years

an exercise *in* joy

You've now been running for more than a few weeks and the initial jolt of inspiration may be wearing off. During your runs this week, pay attention to your feelings and moods about running. Do some of your runs feel hard? On those days, give yourself this pep talk:

This run will feel hard so another run can feel easy.

I may not be able to run as fast or as long as I had hoped today, but that's OK because it's the process of running that matters, not the destination.

I can learn something from every run, even the difficult ones. What can I learn from this one?

Covenant. The revelation may be something as simple as finding a new way to tie your shoelaces so that they stay tight. But every run has the potential to teach you something, to reveal something to you, to be the first time you ever felt a certain way.

I see this most clearly in races. Some runners call it race day magic. It's the extraordinary feeling that occurs when everything comes together. It's the magic that happens when your training coincides precisely with your willingness to push beyond your comfort level on a day that will allow you to do that.

Experienced runners love to tell you about those magic days. For me, one of those magic days was when I ran a PR (personal record) in the 10-K. That day may be the most magic day I'll ever have as a runner. It was the day on which everything came together at the same time. If I run for 50 years and never have another day like that, it will still have been worth it.

How do you stay the course if you're just beginning? It's easier than most people think. In the first few weeks and months, staying the course means avoiding the two most common traps for new runners: unrealistic expectations and impatience. Either of these traps can end your running career before it has a chance to begin.

Unrealistic Expectations

I frequently receive e-mail messages that begin, 'I know I should be able to run faster (or further or easier), but I can't.' Other new runners write to tell me that they *know* they're not progressing as well as they should be. Still others begin by telling me that 'my husband (or wife, brother, sister, friend) says that I should be able to run further by now.'

As soon as I see the word 'should', I know these people are caught in the expectation trap. They've stopped being happy about the progress they're making. They aren't content simply to be on the journey to a fitter, more active lifestyle. They've stopped being the runner they're trying to become and are trying instead to live up to some other set of standards.

These writers often tell me they know that they lack the discipline to get faster or run further. They've convinced themselves or, worse yet, allowed someone else to convince them, that they should be on some 'progress timetable'. The timetable may be a vague, ill-defined one or a schedule they've read or heard about. Whichever it is, they're certain that they're falling further and further behind every day.

Your running won't conform to a timetable. It won't adhere to a schedule that you put on the wall, write in a planning logbook or read in a training book. Your body doesn't care what day of the week it is. Improvement comes over time. You'll get faster and run further when you can – and not a day before.

Impatience

Impatience and unrealistic expectations are similar, although not the same. Expectations are usually driven by something outside of us and are generally negative. Impatience is almost always driven by something internal and may come from a positive source. But the outcome of giving in to your impatience is nearly always a disaster.

Impatience takes many forms. The most common is an unwilling-ness to wait until you're ready for a pace or distance before you take on the challenge. Impatience is wanting to reap the rewards of training before they are fully ripe. I know. I've been there.

lessons learned

I kept putting off getting back into a workout routine because I thought I would hate the obligation. But since the first week, I now look forward to my walks, jogs and weight work. My best tip is to find others, either online or in person, who have similar goals and talk with them, exercise with them and laugh with them.

– Karen Lopez, aged 37 Walking for 36 years (as primary aerobic exercise for 1 year)

It took me 10 months to complete my first marathon. I don't mean that it took me 10 months to prepare for my first marathon. I mean that it took me *10 months* to get from the starting line to the finish line of my first marathon. Why? Because I got impatient.

I'd been running for almost nine months. I'd finished a few 5-Ks and a few 10-Ks. I felt the changes in my body and in my spirit. I was becoming a runner, and I knew it. My only running companion at the time was a friend who was a lifelong runner and marathon runner. He was a few years older than me and had finished over 70 marathons. I took one look at him and signed up for my first marathon. I signed up without a training plan, without a concept of what running a marathon would require, and without a prayer of fin-ishing. And I was off the course by mile seven.

I didn't lack the discipline I needed to train for a marathon. I didn't lack the discipline I needed to line up and face a 26.2-mile racecourse. I had all the discipline I needed to finish the race. I know that now because I've finished 25 of them. What I didn't have then was the dedication I needed to take the time to prepare.

My impatience almost caused me to give up running. It almost cost me the one activity that has given me so much joy. It nearly ruined my life.

It's more difficult to wait patiently while your body and mind go through the changes necessary to be successful at any distance, whether that's running a mile or a marathon. If your impatience causes you to constantly push past your limits or if your impatience with your progress causes you to force your body to do more than it's ready to do, your running will become increasingly less satisfying. On the other hand, if you watch your body change and learn to wait patiently for the next breakthrough, your running will become a constant source of wonder and reinforcement.

It's this mystery that keeps me going. Knowing that on any given day I can be touched by the running gods in a way that takes me to a level I never dreamed I could achieve makes me want to run every chance I get. Giving in to the mystery of my body, of my training and of my soul makes every run an adventure.

When I talk to people who say they used to run but stopped because they were frustrated by their lack of progress, I feel really sad. I wonder if they stopped just one day before the magic might have happened for them. Dedication means not giving up and not giving in. It means not missing the discovery that you were capable of going beyond your wildest dreams if you had run just one more day.

Snakes and Ladders

Training won't always get you what you want, but if you pay attention, you'll usually get what you need

An active lifestyle isn't simply a matter of going in a straight line from where you are to where you want to be, even though it may seem that way at first. The early stages of weekly, even daily, improvement are heady times indeed. But as the months turn into years, being active requires learning to live with the ups and downs of fitness.

After all, most of us have lived long enough to know that life is much more cyclical than linear. We've learned to weather the bad times and relish the good ones.

Becoming active later in life, by which I mean anytime after your teenage years, means accepting the decisions you've made until then as nothing more than decisions you've made. They're not a sentence you have to serve. If you've made poor decisions and are carrying extra weight and a glut of bad habits, it means only that you'll have an easier time identifying what needs to change.

One of the advantages of being horribly out of shape is that it's next to impossible to avoid improvement. In the early months of running, every run is better than the one before. If your first run is only 20 metres long, you have lots of room to improve!

In the early years, almost every race is a personal best. When you finish dead last in your first race, passing even one person in the next race becomes a source of pride. In time, you begin to see the front of the back of the pack. If things go well, you'll soon be able to see the back of the middle of the pack.

Eventually, the weeks and months of steady improvement come to an end. The reality of training, and of the ups and downs of life and running, chip away at the steady momentum of improvement. It's a moment of truth for most new runners.

The Moment of Truth

I'm often asked what the moment of truth was for me. People want to know what provoked me to run in the first place and, more important, why I kept running. The answers are well-documented. I got tired of being fat and out of shape. The honesty of running made it the perfect activity for me.

The real moment of truth didn't come in the early months of running. In fact, the most significant moment of truth came several years into my life as a runner. It was the moment when I first walked off a racecourse, my first DNF (did not finish) – with the exception of the foolish first attempt at a marathon, which I described in the last chapter. That moment has defined me.

It was a very cold December day. At the start line that morning, I wondered about the sanity of starting this race at all. I'd had a difficult autumn that year. I had been injured since a Marathon I had run in early October and I had finished that one by hobbling along on a very sore knee. It wasn't pretty. I still wasn't fully recovered.

This time, I toed the starting line, as I had so many other times, with a strange mixture of excitement and dread. I knew as I stood there that trying to run the marathon was a gamble. I knew I was pushing the limits. I knew, too, that I was pushing my luck.

Around mile 14, the pain in my knee forced me to walk. I had stopped about every mile to try to stretch it out, but to no avail. My plan was to push on regardless, as I'd done the time before. I would finish what I'd started. I wasn't going to quit.

Then, at mile 15, the course turned back towards town and the wind hit me full in the face. The chill I felt went to the bone. About 100 metres ahead I saw a warm police car. I was drawn to the car as if it were a magnet. Before I knew it, I was sitting in the car and asking the officer if she could call the stragglers van for me.

At that moment, I felt less like a runner than I ever had before. Runners ran. Runners – real runners – never quit. Never! I told myself that the injury and pain were just excuses. I had failed.

I was feeling pretty sorry for myself until I got into the stragglers van. Instead of the gloomy bunch of losers I had expected to find, I met a group of runners who were laughing, carrying on and swapping stories about why they had dropped out of the race. They knew then what I was soon to find out: sometimes the best race you can have is the one you don't finish.

> ## lessons learned
>
> *Anyone can walk in races. Yes, you might be last, and yes, someone driving by in a truck might yell, 'Congratulations, you're dead last!' but it will still feel good inside. I knew all I had to do was do it. I spent so many years wishing I could be just like all those other people. I didn't realise I already was just like them. Just an ordinary person.*
>
> **– Linda L. Simmons,**
> **aged 40**
> **Walking for 3½ years**

Hopping into that van was like showing up for a consciousness-raising meeting. I introduced myself and was immediately peppered with questions about why I had stopped running. I explained somewhat sheepishly that my IT band (the iliotibial band, which runs along the outside of your leg from the hip to the knee) had become very painful and that I just didn't want to continue.

'Way to go!' was the universal response. Someone actually applauded my decision, saying, 'Good thinking! You don't want to risk not being able to run for months. No race is worth injuring yourself.'

'What?' I thought in disbelief. 'You mean that sometimes runners *don't* run? You mean that sometimes runners actually respect their bodies enough to *stop* running?' What had been unthinkable moments before became clear: it's running that matters to runners, not one race or one day. Running matters most. Sometimes, the best way to be a runner is to not run.

I started running in December of 1991, but I became a runner in December of 1995 during that unfinished marathon.

Playing the Game

Since that day, I've viewed my running as something I would do for the rest of my life. The pressure was off. I didn't always have to run in order to be a runner. I didn't constantly have to be working towards improvement. I learned that in running, like in life, I'd have some ups and downs. Running could be much more easily integrated into the flow of my life.

I was reminded of the board game Snakes and Ladders that I used to play. It's a simple game. You roll the dice, move your counter around the board, and try to be the first one to reach the finish. The catch is that certain squares allow you to jump ahead one level or several levels, while others drop you back to the previous levels.

Running is really just one giant game of Snakes and Ladders, though in running, there often are more snakes than ladders. You make decent progress in your running and training, and then suddenly an injury sends you back to where you were six months before. So you roll the dice and start again. Improving your running for life means defining improvement differently as you reach different stages in your running.

You can't get faster every time you run. You can't run further every time you put on your shoes. But you can always be a better runner. You just have to learn how to identify and improve the subtle parts of your running that may be obvious only to you.

The Habit of Excellence

The first step in developing a pattern of improvement or the habit of excellence comes with understanding and accepting both the small and large cycles that are present, and necessary, in the life of all runners. It's learning to slide carefully down the snakes and climb relentlessly up the ladders.

By now you know that your training programme must include days of rest and recovery. You know that the training effect occurs not while you're training but while you're recovering. You know that your strength develops during the cycle of stress and rest.

These same principles apply to your running on a larger scale as well. Not only do you need days of rest and recovery, you need weeks or months of rest and recovery. If you've seriously overworked your physical and emotional resources by running, you may need a *year* of rest and recovery.

During a moment of questionable thinking several years ago, I agreed to run two marathons on consecutive weekends. Running a marathon in five hours or so is not that easy for me. Committing to two marathons in two weekends meant devising a training programme that would allow me to get to both starting lines *and* both finish lines. It was a daunting task.

For six months I trained with the discipline and drive of an Olympic athlete. I had a schedule of long runs, tempo runs and speedwork that was as elaborate as a lunar flight plan. I knew what I was going to do on which day several weeks in advance. And I stuck with it.

I trained feverishly through the summer and into the autumn. As the first marathon weekend approached, I applied the same precision

an exercise *in* joy

The first time you must stop a run early, drop out of a race, skip a race altogether or end up finishing much more slowly than ever before, consider it a victory. You're evolving as a runner. Take it in your stride – even boast about it. Allow other runners to learn from your positive attitude.

to tapering that I had to training. I lined up on what turned out to be a perfect marathon day and had a great run.

A week later, I lined up again. That day, the weather was a nightmare. We ran through a steady, cold rain, with wind and cloudbursts and never a glimpse of the sun. I was so tired of running that I put my head down and ran the fastest 10-K of either marathon from mile 20 to the finish. I had done it. I had completed the double.

I didn't train again for almost a year. Oh, I ran. I ran all the time. I ran when I wanted, where I wanted, as long as I wanted, and as far as I wanted. I ran 5-Ks and 10-Ks, even a marathon or two. But I didn't train seriously. After climbing the ladder of training for the 'double', I fell right down the 'snake' of completing them both.

Looking back, I realize that not training during the year following my double was the smartest thing I could have done. Had I decided that there was something more that I needed to do and set a new goal, maybe a triple, I literally would have run myself into the ground. I needed to get away from training and focus my energy on running.

After a year of not training, I began to miss the structure it had given my running. Little by little, I started to train for other events. This time, I trained knowing that at the end of the training cycle, I would go back to running. Knowing that the training cycle had a beginning, a middle and an end added a balance to my total running life that had been missing.

Life in the Fast Lane

You can learn to build in those breaks instead of waiting until your body or your spirit imposes one for you, forcing you to land on a snake. You can decide to take time off, even if that means not running at all, if that will make you a better runner.

The fear that haunts most new runners is that you won't be a runner any more if you stop running. The fear is that if you stop running faster or longer, you'll stop getting better and then you might as well quit forever. It's a fear we all face, one that requires strength to overcome.

lessons learned

Do not listen to your well-meaning friends more than you listen to your body. If a friend says, 'Lengthen your stride,' but you are comfortable with your current stride, ignore him. Your stride will lengthen on its own. If a friend says, 'You need to do speedwork!' but you are excited about running a ¼-mile or a ½-mile and building up a base, ignore her. You will know when you're ready for speedwork. If a friend says, 'You have to breathe only through your nose!' ignore him. Breathe however is easiest and most comfortable for you. And most important, if a friend says, 'Oh, it's OK, run through it,' ignore her. You will learn when your body is ready to be pushed, and you will learn what the 'OK' kind of pain is versus what the 'bad' kind of pain is.

– Rachel Herold, aged 32
Running for 2½ years

It's a groundless fear for most adult athletes. The peak of your running performance, your PR of PRs (the personal record that will remain exactly that – a personal record), lies ahead of you. If you continue to train, your peak performance as an adult runner will occur somewhere between your 7th and 10th year of running.

Your running needn't be all downhill after that. After 7 to 10 years of running, you have a fitness base that will allow you to pursue many other sports and activities. The odds are that you'll be a lifelong athlete. The choice of what to do with the rest of your active life is up to you.

Elite runners face the same fears as those of us in the middle or back of the pack. They want to remain active participants in the sport of running, yet they have to make the same choices and decisions about changes in their performance. They have to choose to accept their movement from the best there is to the best they can be.

Two examples of this ability to enjoy a lifelong career as runners are Amby Burfoot and Bill Rodgers. Amby is longtime editor of *Runner's World* magazine and winner of the 1968 Boston Marathon. When he runs marathons these days, he's often leading a group of runners whose goal is to finish in 4 hours. Amby has remained active and vital in the field of running by focusing his energies on bringing more people into the sport.

Bill Rodgers, four-time winner of the Boston and New York marathons in addition to hundreds of other races, is King of the Roads. Instead of basking in the highlight films of his marathon victories, Bill now races often and hard at shorter distances. No longer fighting for overall trophies, he finds his joy in competing for age-group awards.

Both of these men share a love of running and an understanding of the inescapable truth of the snakes and ladders of their running careers. They know that it's the integrity of the pursuit – years after the public moments of glory – that makes a champion.

You don't have to be a London Marathon winner or a former Olympian to have a running career with ups and downs. You don't have to be an age-group award winner to experience the joy of victory and the agony of defeat. You only have to be a runner for the rest of your life.

The deeper truths about running, the underlying realities of training and ageing, are the same for everyone. In the end, that's what makes it such a great sport. You can't change your fate. You can only choose to accept it with grace or to deny it. But denying it won't change the truth.

How you react the first time that your best isn't as good as it used to be is a defining moment in your running life. All athletes have good days and bad days. Your body won't always give you 100 per cent, despite how much you want it or push it to do so. On some days, you'll do the passing and on others you'll be passed. When you can accept and integrate these principles into your training and racing, you'll be well on your way to running for the rest of your life.

Goal Tending

**The best goals – the ones you'll achieve –
are the ones you can accomplish, revise
and accomplish again.**

The surest recipe for failure is to set unattainable goals, then fail to meet them. It's more important to learn how to set realistic goals and adjust them when necessary than to blindly attempt to meet unrealistic ones. For the new runner, failure is often the result of appropriate enthusiasm combined with inappropriate goals.

Success, and a pattern of success, is learning to accept progress one slow step at a time. The difference between success and failure can be a matter of learning to enjoy the journey, rather than focusing only on the destination.

It's the familiar 'are we there yet' syndrome. When my son was a youngster, he reluctantly conceded to my holiday strategy. With my case of terminal wanderlust, I was happy to be going anywhere. I just wanted to be on the journey.

As is the case with most children, my son wanted to 'be there'. Travelling without a specific goal made no sense to him. 'How will we know when we're getting close to where we're going if we don't know where we're heading?' he would ask. I never had an answer that satisfied him.

It's the same with mature athletes. They want to buy books and follow training programmes that will tell them where they're going to be when they get where they're going. They want to know how to run a faster 5-K or how to run a marathon in under four hours. They want to see models of the bodies that they're going to have. They want concrete examples of people who have been successful.

It's as if the incentive for becoming more active, for running a 5-K or a marathon, or for getting and staying more fit is based on the belief that they'll look and feel like someone else once they've accomplished that goal. They want to escape who and what they are and become someone and something else. The key to unlocking the chains, they believe, is in the goal.

I was no different. When I decided to get fit, I was just as goal focused as any other adult athlete. My first goal was to get off the sofa and out of the house. At least I didn't set too lofty a goal, but for someone who had never exerted himself unless he absolutely had to, getting off the sofa and out of the house was more than a small reach. Getting up and getting out was not a natural behaviour. It required effort.

I did get up and get out. And it felt great – for a while. I congratulated myself for being so disciplined that I could break away from watching television and movie reruns long enough to leave the house. To celebrate my victory over inactivity, I smoked a cigarette. For me, it was a beginning. Unfortunately, my satisfaction with achieving that particular goal was short lived. Getting out of the house wasn't very satisfying after I'd done it a few times.

After ambulating short distances for about a week, I decided on a new goal. I painted a line on the street 1.5 miles from my house. When I got to that line and back, I would have run, walked or waddled for 3 miles. I put that 1.5-mile mark on the road that I travelled to work, so I had to look at it every day. It was calling to me.

Every day I set out for that line. And every day for six months I failed to get there. I failed because I wasn't celebrating the act of running. I wasn't journey focused. Rather, I was goal focused. I failed because I wasn't satisfied with the changes I was making in my life. I failed because I kept my eyes only on the prize, not the process. Looking back, I really don't understand why I kept trying. I don't understand why anyone keeps trying if they're failing every day. And yet, I repeatedly hear new runners say that they aren't running fast enough or far enough every time they run. Not meeting their goal becomes the sum total of their running experience.

The Impossible Goal

We like to think of goals as carrots. We like to think that we use goals as a means to motivate ourselves to succeed. My experience is that too often, we use goals as safety from failure. We know that if we don't meet the goal, we can say we tried and then we can give up.

How often have you set a goal that you *knew* you couldn't meet? You tell yourself that you'll lose 13 kg (2 st) in 10 months or that by a certain date you'll be running 25 miles a week. You tell yourself that having the goal is the best way to stay motivated.

What happens, then, if you don't lose 13 kg or run 25 miles? Having such rigid, specific and quantifiable goals may seem like a good idea at first. But, to be a runner for the rest of your life, you'll have to learn to have goals that are much less precise and much more fluid.

After 6 months of trying, I made it to the line I had painted on the road and back. I ran my 3 miles. When I reached that line and realized that I had failed to fail, I thought I had no choice but to set another goal. This time it was to run a 5-K road race. As before, my underlying (and unadmitted) goal was to find a way to fail so that I could quit.

Much to my surprise and disappointment, I finished the 5-K just fine. It was beginning to appear that I was going to have to continue running if I didn't find a way to fail soon. In fact, I was secretly beginning to enjoy running. I worried that, if I didn't fail soon, I might have to do this forever.

So I picked a 10-K in which to fail. In those days, I wasn't sure exactly what constituted overtraining, so I just ran too fast most of the time. That seemed to keep me sore and slowed me down. But, again, I failed to fail. I finished the 10-K feeling good.

In a near state of panic, I continued training, this time for a half-marathon. Running shoes littered my house, race T-shirts piled up in my cupboard, and my running shorts actually got so old I had to replace them. Anyone looking at my life would think I was a runner. Anyone, that is, except me.

I finally achieved my goal of failing when I decided, after less than a year of running, that the marathon was the ultimate distance for me. Without a nod to those who had run marathons before or a glance at the vast literature on training for them, I devised a training programme that guaranteed failure. At last I had hit on a foolproof way to fail. And fail I did. I wasn't physically prepared to run that distance, and my body gave out on me. I didn't even finish the race.

Setting Goals That Work

It's easy to set goals that are clearly out of reach and then not achieve them. It's easy to ignore the advice and wisdom of people who know better and blindly devise an elaborate plan based on our own ignorance. Failure is often just a matter of showing up unprepared. Succeeding, on the other hand, takes dedication and patience. It requires reason, planning and good judgement.

Can you follow a beginning running programme that is completely devoid of goals? No. Can you begin a running programme that allows for flexibility in goal setting and goal making? Yes.

I use the marathon as a metaphor because I have found no other distance or activity that so closely parallels living for me. I enjoy the flow, the character and the ups and downs of that distance. The lessons I've learned by running marathons are lessons that I've paid for with my body and my spirit.

Standing at the starting line of a marathon, the goal is to run (or walk or run/walk) 26.2 miles. That seems straightforward enough. The goal is precise and well-defined. Or so it would appear. As the miles add up and the distance between the start and finish lines shrinks, the goal changes. You're forced to reevaluate and redefine the simple, single goal with which you began the race.

On good marathon days when everything is working, the weather is right and your training was strong, the goal may be to run the 26.2 miles as fast as possible. That kind of perfect day conjures up visions of a personal record. Your goal becomes not just finishing the course, but running the distance in a specific amount of time. With every mile you recalculate. With every mile the goal changes.

On other marathon days, your goal of running 26.2 miles quickly disappears. As the mile markers pass, you tell yourself that your goal is to run only the miles that are left. You're no longer trying to run 26.2 miles. You are trying to run 22 miles, then 18 miles, then 15. The original goal is lost in the effort of simply trying to complete the course.

On *really* bad marathon days, you can't think about running 26.2 miles. Your goal is to make it to the next mile marker or to run to the next junction or post box. Eventually, your goal becomes no more elaborate than cajoling your legs to take you across the finish line. What started as a goal of running 26.2 miles becomes the goal of taking a single step.

lessons learned

Breathing hard for the first $\frac{1}{4}$-mile or so of any run is normal. It does not mean that you are out of shape. Once your body adapts to the stress, the breathing gets easier. Many people give up the run before their body has a chance to adapt.

– Terry Hickle, aged 48
Running for 35 years

It's true that goals play an important part in helping you track your progress and in keeping you dedicated as a runner. It's just that, to find true joy in running, those goals must be based on your own ability, your own willingness to train and your own metabolism for improvement. And you must become skilled at changing your goals when necessary.

an exercise *in* joy

Examine your goals. Why did you pick them? Are they too lofty or just right? What will you do if you fail to meet them? Remember, a goal is something to work towards, something to help keep you dedicated. But it's the process of working towards the goal that's most important.

Otherwise, you may reach your goals, but you'll miss out on the joys of the journey.

This makes new runners very nervous. They are so unsure of themselves that they think they need a set of external guidelines to assure themselves that they're on the right path. They're convinced that they lack the knowledge, discipline, or tenacity to start a fitness programme and stick with it. They're willing to risk failure in order to not fail.

The best goals are those that are structured into a hierarchy that allows you to build a pattern of achievement. The best goals are the ones that you can accomplish, revise and accomplish again.

If, for example, you go out for your first run and discover that you can't quite run a sub-4–minute mile, what's your next step? Does it make sense to go out again the next day and confirm that you can't run a sub-4–minute mile? And then do it again and again until you have a logbook filled with the evidence of your inability to achieve that goal? No, you would find a more appropriate goal based on your first mile attempt. Let's say you ran that first mile in 7 minutes. Then you might create a new goal of running a 6:55-minute mile, and you'd devise a series of workouts to help you achieve that goal.

Most of us would say that setting an unrealistic goal like running a near–world record time makes *no* sense. Most of us would agree that gauging your progress by such standards is not a good strategy. Yet, we're more comfortable gauging our progress against some equally abstract standard like our brother-in-law, husband or sister. We understand intuitively that we can't compare ourselves to world-class runners at the peak of their careers, but we insist on using people who are more like us as standards.

Defining Your *Own* Standards

Your goals have to be *your* goals. They have to be based on *your* standards. You must judge yourself only by those standards and learn to rely on your own pattern of success as a means of achieving future successes.

If you do, both the rewards and penalties of having goals will be solely yours as well. Setting your own goal and achieving it can be every bit as satisfying as meeting someone else's goal. Of course, failing to meet your own goal can be just as devastating.

One of my most dramatic running failures happened at a marathon in December 2000. I had trained hard that autumn to run a sub-5–hour marathon. I hadn't run a marathon in under 5 hours in almost 2 years, and I wanted to prove to myself that I still could. I'd done all the work necessary to be successful. Working with my coach, I had laid out a training programme that included all the elements of a successful marathon plan. I had a solid base, had done the tempo runs and speedwork, and had run a 26.2-mile run 4 weeks previously.

Lining up in the early morning chill, I was convinced that this was the day. For the first time in over a year I had a specific time goal. For the first time in many years I was prepared to put it all on the line. The weather was good, the course was a fast one and I clicked off the miles one by one, sticking right to my target pace. I was getting the job done. My marathon was going fine … until mile 17.

Without warning, my entire body began to tighten. My legs, arms, hips and feet began to stiffen like setting concrete. It was as if my body had been invaded. By mile 18, my day was over. I hobbled off the course and waved down a car. There wasn't a thing I could do. I could not go on. I sat in the back seat in stunned silence as they drove me to the finish line.

At that point, it didn't matter to me that I had failed to reach a goal that was sub-par by almost every running standard. It didn't matter to me that running a marathon in 5 hours would be considered an awful day for many runners. It didn't matter. It was my goal, and I had failed to achieve it. But the opposite also would have been true. Had I been able to stay on pace and run the marathon in 4:59:59, no one else would have cared. The success, the failure, and the goal itself was of little consequence to anyone but me.

Once I realized that, suddenly I didn't feel so bad about not finishing the race. Realizing that our running goals, and indeed our running itself, are for us alone is a liberating thought. Then, the cold dark mornings aren't about training for a distant goal. They're about the simple joy of getting out there and running. Suddenly, when the run itself is the goal, there are no more bad runs. Suddenly it doesn't matter if we don't finish within our goal time – or don't finish at all. What matters is that we tried, that we enjoyed the process. What matters is that we got out there.

The truth of this came to me early one morning while running with a small group of friends. We had been frolicking through the woods like squirrels in trail shoes when we came upon an athletics field. Covered in dew, the grassy field glistened in the morning sunlight. We stopped long enough to enjoy the scene, then continued our run through the forest. If our goal that morning had been to improve our aerobic capacity, strengthen our quads or quicken our pace, then surely we failed. But our goal that morning was simply to run, to view the world as runners, to experience life in the company of other runners. It was one of the most successful runs any of us could ever have.

Learning to set reasonable and achievable goals was one of the most difficult things for me to learn. It's also one of the most profound lessons that running teaches us. Running can make us stop and consider our goals for today, our goals for ourselves and our goals for our lives. It can teach us that failure is often an illusion and that success can appear when we least expect it.

Beyond Fitness

**Being fit isn't a goal or destination –
it's a way of living life, a natural state**

At some point it finally sank in that I was not going to be able to *get* fit; I was going to have to find a way to *stay* fit. You may think that's obvious, but it wasn't obvious to me. I'd always thought that I would go from being unfit to being fit, and then I'd be done.

The truth is that I never realized that I was staying *un*fit. It never occurred to me that the habits and behaviour that led to my being unfit – the smoking, drinking, overeating and inactivity – were keeping me that way. I thought both fitness and a lack of fitness were static states that you achieved. I now see how wrong I was and how that misconception led me to get increasingly out of shape year after year.

Do you remember the last time you felt fit and were happy in your body? The last time that you felt as though being active were a normal, regular part of your life? Is your memory that good? Mine isn't.

I could dredge up memories of times when I had been active. I had tried playing squash and then tennis for a while; I even tried running for a while. The key was 'for a while'. Even when I was most active, it wasn't for very long.

When I finally realized that being active was something that would have to be a part of my life for the rest of it, I finally was able to secure the dedication needed to stick with a programme. Being fit isn't a destination; it's a way of approaching life. Athletes' lives are defined not by any absolute measure of fitness, but by the means and methods with which they encounter their world.

Effort has a different meaning for athletes. So does the act of sweating, of feeling your heart pounding in your chest. Once you achieve a level of fitness that allows you to celebrate the effort that your body is capable of, I can't imagine that you'll ever want to give that up.

For me, the process of staying fit has meant running and walking. I've chosen to stay with these modes for many reasons. First and foremost, I really like running and walking. Second, running or walking is about the most convenient form of exercise I can think of. Last, but not least, I like being around other runners. Their values are the same as my values.

It's not *just* running and walking that I enjoy, though. I love to ride bicycles. I enjoy occasionally paddling a canoe or strapping on a pack and hiking for a day. Being fit has meant that I've been able to be playful and to take on new challenges. The surprising part is that I enjoy being fit so much that it's sometimes enough to just sit still.

It's hard to believe that inactivity is an important part of an active lifestyle, but it is. I have a friend who *times* his rest sessions with the same precision that he times his workout sessions. He's as serious about his inactivity as he is about being active. This strategic inactivity may come as a shock to your friends and family, so be prepared for their incredulity. The first time they realize that you're timing your naps with your running watch, they may want to have you committed. Tell them it's part of a very complicated training programme that would take too long to explain, and then go back to napping.

The Next Step

There comes a time when even die-hard runners want to move beyond the next training session, 5-K, or marathon to something else. Almost anything seems possible once you begin to see past your limitations. When you've achieved what was once unthinkable, you have to look beyond the next finish line.

This seems especially important to those of us who became active later in life. I never expected to be in the kind of shape I'm in at this age, in my mid-50s. I thought I'd be spending my days sitting comfortably behind a desk and my nights sitting comfortably in front of the TV at this stage in my life. I expected *all* life's active moments to be in my past.

lessons learned

Even if it feels cold outside, you will get very warm while running, even if the pace is slow. Don't overdress. CoolMax T-shirts, socks and tights are a lot more comfortable than cotton when wet.

– Lauren Clark, aged 44 Running for 2 years

The real fun started for me when I accepted that being fit was my natural state. The whole world of activity opened up to me when I accepted that being able to walk and run was something I could assume I could do. Suddenly it seemed that there was nothing that I *couldn't* do.

I was wrong again, of course. There are lots of things I can't do – many activities and sports that require skills I don't have. But I discovered that the patience and tenacity I had developed as a runner was a big asset in taking on new challenges.

Accepting the challenge of trying a new activity or sport can fuel your interest in running. It all works together. Learning a new skill can rekindle your passion for improving your running and translate into a more effective running programme.

For example, in the summer of 2000, I ran a half-marathon that began at around 1,800 m (6,000 ft) above sea level and went to about 4,300 m (14,000 ft). You not only have to cover the distance, you have an 1,800-m (8,000-ft) vertical gain to climb. As a flatlander, I couldn't prepare for this event by running at elevation, so I was faced with the need to devise a training plan that would do everything except acclimatize me to the altitude. (I didn't, by the way, accept the training advice of a running friend who told me that the way to get ready was to get on a treadmill, set the grade to its highest percentage, put a plastic bag on my head and a rubber band around my neck, and then walk until I passed out!)

My training plan included three new elements that weren't completely foreign to me, but which hadn't been part of my regular training pattern: trail running, hill hiking (with a loaded pack) and hill climbing on a mountain bike (with a loaded pack).

I had run a little on paths and trails but never felt it was part of my identity as a runner and road racer; to include it as an element of my training programme was a new concept. I was one of those runners who liked to pound the pavement. I liked to feel my foot hitting a solid surface. The goal of trail running was to prepare for the uneven terrain that I would face on the hill climb. During the very first trail running session, I could tell where the weakest parts of my body were. It was clear I needed to strengthen my ankles and the muscles that stabilize my knees.

The point of hill hiking with a loaded pack was, again, to strengthen the 'pushing' parts of my legs without putting a lot of stress on my joints and tendons. By simulating the kind of low speed, high effort movement that I was likely to face, I also was preparing mentally as well as physically.

Hill climbing on the mountain bike was intended to build even greater strength with even less risk. Grinding up a hill on the bike was physically exhausting, but it was an activity that wasn't as likely to lead to injury.

I incorporated these activities in my training programme because I wanted to have a better race. I began doing them because I was a runner, and, as a runner, I wanted to have a better experience 'running' the ascent. But before long I began to enjoy the activities in their own right, not solely for their benefits to my training programme.

an exercise *in* joy

During your next run, walk, bike ride or swim, focus on the joy of activity. Forget about the calories you're burning and the cholesterol you're lowering. Just focus on the feeling of movement. Feel the sun or wind on your skin. Smell the trees and flowers. Listen to the birds. See the light and the shadows. Even when you are not moving, focus on how being fit allows you to feel. Feel the tautness of your muscles, the energy in your step, the power in your lungs. Feel the joy of being fit.

I discovered that I really liked trail running – probably because being slow on the trails isn't as obvious as being slow on the pavement. My low centre of gravity, which was of no use on the streets, was a big advantage on the trails. And I was much better at reading the trail than I thought I would be.

I began to look forward to the trail running workouts. They became an integral part of my normal running, rather than something I did outside of it. And the trail running helped improve my street running. As my ankles grew stronger, my feet became more stable. As the muscles around my knees strengthened, there was less stress on the knee joints. It was amazing.

The hiking, too, became something I enjoyed beyond its contribution to my running. Hiking along trails and ridges that I would never have dared run introduced a realm of the outdoors that I never would have experienced otherwise.

Mountain biking reawakened a joy I hadn't felt since I was a young boy pedalling at breakneck speeds (on an old bike with spring suspension) through forest near the city suburbs. These new activities, which

I began as a supplement to my running, became new ways to bring meaning to my life as an athlete.

Living an Athlete's Life

The revelation that you're living an active lifestyle doesn't hit you all at once. It edges into your consciousness over time. The acknowledgement that you're an athlete – moving in an athlete's body and living in an athlete's world – is something you bestow on yourself. When you do, the world becomes a giant adult playground to which you have the key.

We live in a time that affords us almost unlimited opportunities to become fit and stay active. Every day I read about a new sport that has entered the national consciousness. As I write this, I'm convinced someone out there is coming up with the next great activity. With the possible exception of bungee jumping and skydiving, I'm ready to try whatever it is that he or she comes up with.

We've learned from our running that we can't expect to be very good at a new activity right off the bat, so we approach each new sport with the perspective gained from logging all those miles. When we hop on a bike or strap on in-line skates, we know what it will take to get better.

We're also well aware that the only reason to try any new sport is to enjoy the learning process, to get personal satisfaction from the new activity when we try to overcome our fears and inabilities, and because we expect it to be fun. We did it once, with running, so we know we can do it again with another activity.

Cross-training

Much has been written about the benefits of cross-training. Everything from strength training to yoga is touted as the way to become a better runner. I agree: anything that helps you think about yourself as a runner and athlete is a good thing.

So who needs to cross-train? Everyone – new runners, experienced runners, young runners, old runners, men, women, long-distance runners, short-distance runners. You don't cross-train instead of running; you cross-train because you're a runner.

What's the best cross-training activity for runners? That's a little like asking how many miles a week you should run and what your pace should be. The same answer won't work for everyone. And the right answer for you today may not be the right answer for you a year from now.

It's difficult, however, to underestimate the benefits derived from even a modest strength-training programme. I'm not talking about 'pumping up'. I'm talking about the kind of programme that will build your core body strength and eliminate strength imbalances.

We learned earlier that muscles are very specific in the way they do their jobs. They're also very specific in what they don't do. Running will build strength and endurance only in those muscles you use while running. The more years and miles you log as a runner, the greater the strength disparity becomes between your running muscles and your non-running muscles. Also of particular benefit to women, strength training will preserve bone density in addition to muscle.

Other forms of cross-training are very effective as part of a lifetime fitness programme. Cycling, rowing and stair or wall climbing are a few that can keep your running programme varied and interesting. The beauty, as a runner, is that you can rotate through different kinds of cross-training and still reap the benefits. (For more information about different cross-training activities, see the next chapter.)

Fit for Life

Can you *get* fit? No! You can get to work; you can get to the church on time; but you can't *get* fit. Fitness isn't a state of being that you achieve, then relax and enjoy. A holiday is a state of being that you achieve, then relax and enjoy. Fitness is a never-ending process.

However fit you are today, a year from now you will be either more or less fit. The choice is up to you. If you maintain your current level of activity, you'll probably be at roughly the same level of fitness you are today, allowing for the inevitable changes related to ageing. All of our biological clocks are ticking. The slow, relentless ravages of time and gravity work their tricks on our bodies.

Moving past your initial fitness goals means giving in to the joy of being active. It means forgetting that you started an active lifestyle specifically to lose weight and lower your cholesterol. It means accepting that you're feeling better and having more fun than you ever imagined was possible at your age. It means accepting that you've won the most difficult race you'll ever run – the race against time.

Your joy in activity won't be an adult joy. It will be the joy children feel when they run across a field of wild flowers or through a lawn sprinkler on a hot summer day. Eventually you'll forget that your heart is getting stronger and your lungs are working better. All the adult reasons fade quickly when you can't wipe the smile off your face.

lessons learned

It's not easy. It's going to take more time than you thought. You can't do it alone. Someone will give you support, and you need to be thankful to them for that support. You have to learn how to quiet the voice in your head that says, 'You're hot. You're tired. Your legs are dead. This is crazy. Why don't you stop?'

**– Bill Hermann, aged 51
Running for 6 years**

Basic Truths about

Cross-training

Everything you need to know about cross-training and living fit for the rest of your life

If you're a brand-new runner, you may not believe that some day you'll want to do more than run. But you will. Once you've discovered how much fun it is to be fit and active, you'll want to find as many ways as possible to keep moving and to enjoy your new fitness level.

No one was more surprised than me when, at 43 years old, I found myself standing waist deep in a cold lake early one September morning, wearing Speedos and staring nervously at an island a half-mile away. The plan was to swim to the island and back as the first leg of a triathlon, ride a bike for 25 miles, then run for 6.2 miles. This was *me*, the same person who was smoking more than a pack a day 9 months earlier.

Except for the Speedos I felt pretty good about doing a triathlon. If you've lost weight, you'll understand. I was about 36 kg (5½ st) lighter, but I still had all that extra skin. It wasn't pretty. But what better way to strengthen my dedication to my new lifestyle than to take on a new challenge? Running had already become much more than a way to maintain my cardiovascular fitness. It had become a means of exploring a whole new world of athletics.

The lesson to be learned from cross-training is that there are many things you can do to improve your running that have absolutely nothing to do with running. That's the good news. The days of pounding out 140-mile weeks in order to call yourself a runner are long gone, even for most élite athletes. Contemporary runners understand that the body responds best to a mixture of specific and comprehensive training.

As the term is used here, cross-training means other activities that you *like* to do, that you *want* to do, and that you *can* do that also enhance your running performance. Cross-training isn't an activity that you do *instead* of running (unless you're recovering from an injury), but rather, an activity you do *because* you're a runner.

Some types of cross-training are better for your running than others. For example, some specifically strengthen and stretch muscles that will help build your running speed and endurance. Others help by simply giving your running muscles a break, the time they need to rest and recover. All cross-training activities are important because they round out your fitness, help you control your weight, prevent injuries and enhance your enjoyment of running and fitness in general.

It's impossible to cover every possible form of cross-training here, so use your imagination and explore your own interests to identify other activities you might enjoy. You may want to do some of these once a week, some once a month, and still others only once a year. How often you engage in the activity isn't as important as understanding that, as an active person, you *can* do them.

Strength Training

Strength training may enhance your running and overall well-being more than any other fitness pursuit. You'll notice that I use the term 'strength training,' not 'weightlifting'. You lift weights, but that's not the goal. You lift weights to get stronger in order to be a better runner.

You may think of weightlifting, or even strength training, as a body building activity intended for people who want to 'pump-up' or sculpt their bodies with muscles. It's true that body builders lift weights, but so do runners. The difference lies in how they focus their lifting programme.

Old-school runners, the beanpole types from the 1970s, would never have considered strength training as a way of becoming better runners. They were very much like some of the musicians I worked with who did nothing but practise their instruments 7 or 8 hours a day. They were so consumed by the activity itself that they believed engaging in the activity was the only way to improve.

We now know better. We know that, next to the actual time you spend running, strength training is the most important cross-training activity you can do. Anecdotal evidence and formal research indicates that a solid strength-training programme for runners will build the lean muscle mass that burns the most calories, reduces the risk and rate of injury and helps make you faster.

Strength training can improve your running form by reducing muscle imbalances. Runners tend to have very strong hamstrings but weak quadriceps. The resulting imbalance can lead to knee pain and injury. The cure and the prevention is strength training.

Contrary to the old-school common wisdom that strength training makes you tight and inflexible, many runners find that a resistance-training programme is actually a good form of flexibility training. Using resistance (free weights or machines) takes your muscles gently through their full range of motion. The result is not only a stronger muscle but one that is functioning closer to its full potential.

Runners, especially women, worry that they will 'bulk up' from weight training. Don't worry; you won't end up looking like Mr or Ms Universe. It's not going to happen using a strength-training programme designed for runners or in the limited time you'll devote to this form of cross-training.

To be most effective, you need to strength train at least twice a week. Some evidence suggests that once a week works, but twice a week is better and three times a week is ideal. Develop a programme that includes both upper- and lower-body exercises. Many runners think they can ignore strengthening their lower bodies since they get so much exercise running, but one of the biggest benefits of lower-body strength training is to correct the imbalance between your hamstrings and quadriceps that develop with running. Here's a sample programme that you can do at home or at a commercial gym with dumbbells and a bench.

lessons learned

It's important to 'schedule' rest days into your training and not feel guilty for taking time off to let soreness go away and allow muscles to recover. Rest is as important to training as the running or walking itself, and it takes time to find out for oneself how many days per week one can run without raising one's risk of injury.

**– Carol Schobert, aged 48
Running for 5 years**

1. Pushup. These oldies-but-goodies work your chest and triceps. If you lack the upper-body strength, start by doing pushups with

your knees on the ground. When you're ready, advance to doing them on the balls of your feet.

2. Pullup. Don't get scared. Few people can do these, but the act of trying is a great shoulder and back workout. Set up a pullup bar or rock-climbing apparatus (sold at sporting goods stores). If you can't do a full pullup, place a bench under the bar and use it to kick yourself into the up position, lowering yourself as slowly as possible. Try to hold yourself up with your arms bent at various angles. Eventually you'll be able to do a full pullup.

3. Double crunch. You need strong abs for good running posture. To save time, try crunching your shoulders and hips towards each other, working both your upper and lower abdominals simultaneously.

4. Lunge. These are great because they work just about every muscle in your legs and buttocks. For the basic lunge, step forward with your right leg and sink your buttocks down until both your right and left leg form right angles. Then push yourself back up. Once you feel comfortable with the basic lunge, try walking lunges where you move from one end of the room to another.

5. Superman. Lie on your belly and contract your abs and rear end as you raise your outstretched hands and feet off the ground. Hold for a few seconds and then repeat. This will strengthen your lower back.

This programme will work most of the major muscles in your body by using your body weight and dumbbells as resistance. You can also use machines, bands, tubes or tins of beans if you prefer. And there are literally hundreds of exercises to choose from. How you get stronger isn't as important as *that* you get stronger.

Cycling

I started biking before I started running. I knew my joints wouldn't tolerate the pounding of running before I lost some of the weight, so I bought myself a second-hand 10-speed, stuck my feet into those toe-clips and set off down the road.

It wasn't fun at first. The inventor of those toeclips should be found and punished. If you get your foot in there tight enough to do any good, you can't get it out when you need to stop. I've still got pieces of gravel in my elbow from the 30 or 40 times I fell over, usually at traffic lights in front of a truckload of hooting building workers or a car full of attractive young women.

Cycling, like running, is enjoying a resurgence of interest among the general population. The days of the 'roadies' – when packs of 5 to 50 cyclists dressed in electric-coloured, skin-tight, matching outfits blew by on the bike path at speeds exceeding 25 miles per hour – are gone. You still see a few bikers out there in their Tour de France outfits, but not so many. The phase when everyone thought they had to have a mountain bike with 48 speeds, knobby tyres, and a saddle position that put their rear ends about 1 metre above their shoulders seems to have passed, too. I was always amused to see someone riding a bike designed for 65-mph downhill racing on the local bike path.

Biking, again like running, has returned to its roots. It's a fun, economical way to get from here to there. You don't have to spend a lot of money on a lot of fancy equipment. You just need a bike with two wheels, pedals and a saddle that's comfortable to ride.

The beauty of biking for a runner is that it strengthens the quadriceps, the very muscles you need for good knee health. Best of all, you get a quality cardiovascular workout without putting any weight on your lower joints.

lessons learned

I have been learning a multitude of good things in the course of my 12 years of racewalking, so it's hard to focus on one. But the first thing I learned was the importance of good shoes. I learned that by experience. I walked my first 5-miler in cheap gym shoes and when I finished, my heels were all black and blue.

– Charles Cohn, aged 68
Racewalking for 12 years

If you choose to bike, be careful about setting the saddle height correctly so that you don't risk injuring your knees. The easiest way to get close to the right saddle height is to pedal with your heels, setting the saddle height at the point where your heels just rest on the pedals. Then, when you pedal with your feet, the extra length of your foot should take all the pressure off your hips and knees.

Like traditional cycling, stationary biking (called Spinning) is an excellent way to build complementary muscles, get additional low-risk cardiovascular workouts and stay 'fit' while taking time off from running. An organized Spin class, for example, is a great way to get in a social workout.

Elliptical Training

These devices work a little like riding a bicycle while standing upright, or like cross-country skiing without using your arms. The motion of your feet is, well, elliptical, and there is no impact at all.

Inspirational
Tools of the Trade

Before you turn the page, make sure your dedication is firm by doing the following:

1. Work at least one day of cross-training into your weekly routine.
2. Find at least one joyful reason to run that doesn't centre on weight loss, speed, competition or health.
3. Examine your goals, making sure they are realistic and uniquely yours.
4. Accept the fact that some runs will be uphill, whereas others will be down, regardless of the actual terrain.

I've tried an elliptical trainer several times and have concluded that I simply don't have the coordination to get an effective workout from this machine. I spent most of my time scared to death. But many runners use it and claim that it's a great way to get in additional weight-bearing, non-impact training.

Elliptical trainers are the saviours of many injured runners because they come closest to simulating the motion of running without actually putting impact on your muscles or joints. Go slowly at first, to get used to the machine. Then you can try to speed up your gait. Eventually you can set the foot 'pedals' at different levels of resistance and tilt to simulate running up- and downhill.

Stairclimbing

I'm partial to stairclimbing because the machine I used had huge platforms for your feet, made just enough noise to impress everyone in the gym, and if you put in a number twice your weight, the 'calories used' display was amazing to watch. But it was also a great workout.

The stairclimber will help you remedy muscle imbalances and allow you to feel those imbalances better than running does. You can alter the intensity of the stairclimber easily, frequently and over a wider range of intensity or difficulty levels than you can while running. If the machine has programmemable workouts, you can 'set it and forget it' while you reap the benefits.

Rowing

Rowing is an excellent way to improve upper body strength and coordination. Don't just jerk the 'oars' back and forth. Try to fluidly row them using your legs, back and arms. Developing and maintaining good rowing form increases your arms and upper body strength as well as your 'core' body strength around the upper and lower back.

Cross-country Skiing (or Simulating)

Not long ago, I was on a winter trek. As I patted myself on the back for getting out in the cold and snow to get in a solid training session, a cross-country skier flew by me with sweat flying off of every bodily surface. *He* was getting a solid training session much more than I was.

It's hard to beat cross-country skiing for overall biomechanical and cardiovascular effectiveness. Almost every muscle in your body gets used in one way or another. At the calmest pace, cross-country skiing ranks very high as a method of enhancing your running performance. But there's no reason you have to wait until your winter holiday to get in this workout.

To be honest, though, I have the same problems getting the hang of the cross-country ski simulator that I have with the elliptical trainer. I always seem to have both arms forwards when both legs are back. Again, if *you* can make it work, you'll get in a great workout to enhance your running.

Swimming

I mentioned earlier that I've done several triathlons. Swimming was both the most satisfying and frustrating aspect of triathlon training. There's nothing quite like the peace and calmness of swimming to clear your head, but it was frustrating because at my best I swam as if I had blocks of concrete tied to my hips and ankles.

If you get beyond going back and forth in the pool without drowning, swim training can be an excellent way to improve your aerobic fitness, your upper body strength, your muscular endurance and your breath control. And, for what it's worth, it doesn't take long to teach yourself to breathe *only* when your mouth is actually *out* of the water. Swimming is also an excellent alternative to stretching as a way to maintain your flexibility.

Water Running

Most runners consider water running an option only when they're injured. The prospects of wearing a Styrofoam vest and pretending to run back and forth across the deep end of a swimming pool is about as exciting as watching paint dry. But for the uninjured, and especially the new runner, water or pool running is an excellent form of cross-training.

The obvious advantage and the reason to water run when you're injured is that it's non–weight bearing and has no impact. An added advantage for every runner is that you can work on your running form without risking injury. Your running inefficiencies become much more obvious in the water than when you're running on a path or track.

For example, if you have a tendency, as I did, to circle rather than bring your leg straightforward during the running motion, you'll spot it immediately in the water. If your arms flail aimlessly about you – the water will make that obvious. If you have a little problem with your legs you'll be able to see and correct it much faster in the water.

Treadmill Running

The treadmill is an essential part of every new runner's training routine. You can measure both your pace and distance with precision on a treadmill, and you can stop immediately if you need to.

The treadmill, like water running, also allows you to get instant feedback when you make changes in your running style. You can alter your gait, lengthen or shorten your stride, play with your breathing and see the result of the changes on the treadmill display. You can focus on changing single aspects of your running form, like breathing or arm movement, one at a time without distraction.

The treadmill is a great place to test shoes, too. I go to the gym with a bag full of different pairs of shoes. I run with one pair, switch, and then switch again. I run with different shoes on my left and right feet. I try different socks with different shoes. I change the insoles, trying various over-the-counter brands. The treadmill is the perfect place to detect subtle differences in shoes and to determine which works best for you. The differences in cushioning, support, stability, shape and size between shoes quickly becomes obvious in comparing them while running short distances on the treadmill.

Trekking and Walking

I was once asked what the difference is between trekking and walking. I made up something about the subtle differences in goals and equipment, but the truth is, I'm not sure. For the purpose of cross-training, I'm talking about any form of moving yourself while standing on your own two feet that doesn't involve running.

While the act of walking is not identical to running, it does produce some of the same movements in your muscles, joints and tendons. The big difference, of course, is that there is much less impact during walking or trekking, so you can engage in the activity for much longer periods of time without worrying about the risk of an overuse injury.

My mother is a die-hard race walker. You've probably seen race walkers on the track with their arms pumping and their hips wiggling. Do yourself a favour – don't make fun of them. At 68, my mum out-walked me in a 5-K. I was sore for a week from moving all those new muscles. You don't need to go to the extreme of race walking to get the benefits, but the fluid, non-impact race walking form can make you a smoother, more efficient runner.

Trekking, with or without a backpack and with or without trekking poles, will help strengthen your ankles, knees and hips; improve your balance and stamina; and develop the mental toughness you'll need for longer races as your running endurance increases. The loaded backpack increases your strength and the poles help to maintain correct posture on longer treks, so don't be afraid to use such equipment.

Climbing

You may have seen a climbing wall in some of the bigger sporting speciality stores and thought, 'No way! I can't do that.' I'm here to tell you that you can.

The kind of rock or wall climbing that I'm interested in allows you to see the entire puzzle of the climb, then work out the best path to the top. It's also more about coordination and lower body strength than about being able to hang by your fingers. Most stores offer instruction and a chance to experience a climb. My advice is to try it.

Paddling

If you think of kayaking as being trapped in a tiny boat that's hurling towards rocks in a foaming whitewater river, you've watched too much television. The kind of kayaking that makes for exciting television is beyond the skill and sense of most of us, but, like running and biking, kayaking has a saner, more sensible side.

Modern kayaks are available in inflatable and 'sit-on' styles. They don't require that you sit inside with a protective skirt around your waist. Both the inflatable and sit-on kayaks permit you to simply hop off if the going gets rough or if the boat begins to capsize. Also, if you kayak on flat water, as opposed to a river, you'll encounter very little obstacles to tip you over. Like its cousin, the canoe, the two-person kayak can be the perfect way to spend time on a quiet lake enjoying the serenity of the surroundings, and it's an excellent way to enjoy the benefits of being fit and active.

If you want to try river kayaking, first take a class to learn how to 1) read the currents, 2) safely exit your kayak if it tips, and 3) learn basic safety procedures. Most important, only attempt rivers at your skill level. Most rivers are rated in difficulty on a scale of one (easy) to six (only those with a death wish should try it). The difficulty level may change over the year depending on rainfall and water releases (when dams allow more water through than usual).

Orienteering

Although it may seem more like an elaborate treasure hunt than a serious cross-training activity, orienteering can be the perfect combination of learning new skills, getting outdoors and spending time on your feet.

Imagine being given a map and compass and told to find 10 to 20 'checkpoints' over a 5- to 6-mile course. Being fit isn't enough. You must use your body and mind together in orienteering. Whether you do it alone or with a team, it's sure to put a smile on your face as you do your best wilderness scout imitation.

The Spice of Life

Beyond the many fitness benefits, cross-training and participating in other sports can keep your running fresh and new for the rest of your life. Running becomes the foundation of your active lifestyle, rather than something you do to counteract the effects of gravity and ageing.

Nothing is quite so much fun as trying a new sport with a new attitude. Biking for fun or paddling for pleasure takes the definition of fitness to a new level, and your running takes on a whole new character. It becomes a partner in your exploration of life.

Recommended Reading

▶ Anderson, Bob, Ed Burke, Bill Pearl and Richard Golueke. *Getting in Shape: Workout Programmes for Men and Women*. Bolinas, CA: Shelter Publications, 1995.

▶ Couch, Jean. *The Runner's Yoga Book: A Balanced Approach to Fitness*. Berkeley, CA: Rodmell Press, 1990.

▶ Moran, Gary T. and George H. McGlynn. *Cross-Training for Sports: Programmes for 26 Sports*. Champaign, IL: Human Kinetics, 1997.

▶ Pearl, Bill and Gary T. Moran. *Getting Stronger: Weight Training for Men and Women*. Bolinas, CA: Shelter Publications, 1986.

▶ Peterson, James A., Cedric X. Bryant, and Susan L. Peterson. *Strength Training for Women*. Champaign, IL: Human Kinetics, 1995.

▶ Siler, Brooke. *The Pilates Body: The Ultimate At-Home Guide to Strengthening, Lengthening, and Toning Your Body – Without Machines*. New York, NY: Broadway Books, 2000.

Part 4
Celebration

Finding the Joy

Focus on where you are instead of where you wish you were. The joy will follow

I freely admit that I've looked forward to writing the next four chapters more than any of the previous. After all the talk about why to be active, when to be active and how to be active, I get to write about the payoff of being active, about the joy and celebration of it all.

There's no reason to do any of it – to run, walk or race – unless it brings joy into your life. You can find satisfaction in the act of moving your body from the first tentative steps. There's no need to postpone the joy until you've reached a dreamt up point of experience or skill. As a beginner, the time to find and embrace the joy is now.

Despite all the public exposure to 'The Penguin' philosophy, I'm still asked why someone who has as little talent as I have wants to compete in road races. And it's not always a former skinny-fast, age-group award winner who poses this question. More often than not it's someone, like me, who can't figure out how to enjoy something they're not good at.

The answer to the question can be found at almost any road race. Those who doubt the power of personal achievement need only stand at the finish of a local 5-K and watch the first-timers cross the line.

You'll see in their eyes what you'll see in mine: pure, unmitigated, unrestrained joy.

I once spent several hours at the finish line of a large major marathon, cheering as the back of the pack participants finished in 5, 6 or more hours. I watched their faces as they crossed the timing mat. I watched their bodies as they succumbed to the fatigue. I watched their souls as they gave in to the reality of their accomplishment.

Some people finished in a state of suspended animation. They looked as if the world had suddenly come to a complete standstill. They crossed the finish line and just stopped, waiting for someone, anyone, to tell them what their next step should be.

Others crossed the finish line angry. I could only guess at whom the anger was directed – a hyper-critical parent, an unsupportive partner, an unrelenting childhood bully, a dictatorial boss. They finished with fists clenched and arms pummelling the air, as much in defiance as in celebration.

Still others finished crying. The tears began the moment these runners realized that they were going to finish the marathon. From that instant, they began to release the doubts and fears that drove them to

lessons learned

I was so embarrassed about how I looked (chubby) and what people would think of me. What I found out was that people just seemed so impressed that I had just got out there. It didn't matter what I looked like or whether I came in last at a race. I got support.

Entering a race was such a great experience. I will never forget the feeling the first time I ran across a finish line. I may have been last, but I got cheers and the knowledge that I had done something good for myself. I knew that day that I would keep running.

– Jeanette Lampron, aged 53
Running for 5 years

begin training, the same doubts and fears that often paralyzed them in other areas of their lives. The finish line was like a commencement ceremony for them – a beginning rather than an end.

But the emotion I saw on the faces of the vast majority of first-time marathon runners as they crossed the finish line was joy – real, honest, earned joy. It was joy that they could see, feel and believe in, that they could cling to. It was theirs alone. It can never be taken away from them.

I'm afraid the cynics who wonder why I race have never seen that joy. If they had, they wouldn't question my reasons, or anyone's right, to experience that joyful satisfaction with themselves and their efforts.

Beyond wondering why I race, some people question why I continue to run at all, given my abject lack of genetic ability. These doubters believe the myth that expertise and enjoyment are inseparable. These people believe that only the truly talented, highly skilled and most gifted runners should reap the rewards of participation. They don't like my answer to why I bother running. I tell them it's simple. I continue to run because I like running. I like to run even though I'm not, by their standards, any good at it. What matters to me is that I like to run, not what they think about my running. Maybe it's a '60s thing – 'Power to the Penguins!'

Understanding that I could find joy in the activity itself, rather than in my level of proficiency, liberated me. Imagine the number of physical activities you might engage in if you didn't care how good you were. Imagine the other goals you might pursue if you didn't have to wait until you were 'good at it' to begin to enjoy the pursuit.

Had I pursued all my dreams, my life would be overflowing with the evidence of my successes at having attempted them rather than with the remnants of my failures. My walls would be covered with photographs that I took and liked – until I found out they weren't really all that good. I would probably sit at my piano and play Beethoven's 'Moonlight Sonata' with clumsy fingers, not caring that the notes and rhythm weren't perfect.

My life would be cluttered with tiny trophies – the kind you give yourself, not the kind you win – from the past 50 years, not just the nine years since I've been running. I would have patches from places I'd been, mugs from events I'd entered, and T-shirts from races I'd finished.

Your Best *Is* Good Enough

It isn't easy to find the joy at first. I took the same adult attitudes that had served me so well as a professional musician, academic faculty member, administrator and businessman into my life of activity. I had been successful at those endeavours by not accepting my limitations, by not accepting anything less than the best. Not *my* best, mind you, *the* best.

When I started running, I identified the standards in the field and immediately began to move towards accomplishing them. In the best Total Quality Management fashion, I benchmarked. I found out how fast *fast* was for someone my age and decided I would achieve that same speed. I read the results pages in the local running club newsletter to see how fast the *best* runners in my age group were and planned a pro-gramme so that I could be better. I thought I could train my way to the front of the pack.

Once again, I was wrong. It doesn't work that way for most of us, especially mature athletes. If we've squandered away our young adult-hood and a good bit of our middle age, it's a shock to find out what excellence in our age group means. A few jolts to the ego may be nec-essary before we accept that no amount of desire or effort will get us to that level.

Even when it became painfully clear that I would never be among the leaders, I clung desperately to the hope that I could at least be in the hunt. Alas, it wasn't to be. Only when I began to respect the talent and skill of my competitors was I able let go of my own unrealistic expectations.

Then what? What do you do when the truth of your indiscretions and the weight, both literally and figuratively, of your previous lifestyle decisions hit you squarely in the face? You have two choices. You can

an
exercise
in **joy**

What do you have to feel joyful about? Take a moment and think about all the wonderful things running has brought you during your journey as a runner. Do you look and feel better? Have you experienced the world in a new way, seeing flowers and scenery for the first time on foot? Take a moment to celebrate. You have a lot to feel good about.

either cave in to the fear that you have already ruined your life, or, you can start where you are and enjoy the process of getting to where you're going.

The first choice, caving in, is the easier of the two. We look at ourselves at age 30, 40 or 50 and see all the evidence we need to justify caving in. We see a belly where our waist used to be. We can't see our feet. We struggle to walk up the steps or play with our children. We look in the mirror and see more of what we are and less of what we want to be. Many of us get trapped in our own bodies. We're prisoners of what I call 'sedentary confinement'. Worse, we are our own guards and governers. We are the ones who won't commute our sentences.

The alternative – facing and accepting the truth without self-judgement and then making a realistic, achievable plan for living an active lifestyle – is much more difficult. It means forgiving and forgetting a lot. It means finding new ways to experience our bodies and our selves.

I turned inside, to a part of me that had only escaped on holidays. At the centre of my being, I'm a process person. I like the 'getting there' part of a holiday much more than the 'being there' part. Once I've arrived, it seems like I'm already half-way back. Tapping into that 'process person' meant that it didn't matter where I was starting my new life. It didn't matter how much I weighed, how out of shape I was, what size trousers I was wearing, or how many years I had ignored my body's need to move. I was going to start where I was and move to where I wanted to be.

Tapping into the process meant finding the joy in the activity even while I wasn't being active. It meant smiling when I saw that my running shoes were getting a little worn. It meant passing on a dessert because I knew I was going to run later in the day. It meant taking better care of myself because I wanted to be a better runner.

Finding Joy in the Journey

At first, much of the joy in running comes during the times when we're not running at all. The joy comes in planning our runs, calculating the time and distance it will take, thinking about the last run, anticipating the next one. In fact, for someone who starts where I did, it's much easier to find the joy in running when you're not running than when you are.

That changes over time. The struggle to run 25 metres without hacking, coughing and feeling like you need to die in order to feel better isn't much fun at first. You worry about what other people think when they see you running, that they're undoubtedly wondering what in the world you think you're doing. It's not easy to take the results of a life of indiscretions and put them on public display. I advise new runners to smile when they run. It confuses the people who are watching!

We can all tap into the joy-in-motion part of our spirits by letting go of the need for a destination. When we reject the obsession with what we wish we were and focus on what we are, the joy will follow. When I stopped looking at myself as the fat old man who ran and saw instead the *runner* who was a fat old man, the joy in my spirit began to explode. The joy came from being a runner. Yes, I was a runner who had started late in life. I was a runner who had begun running with 36 extra kilos of weight. I was a runner who couldn't run 50 metres. But I *was* a runner.

The other labels I used to define myself would change in time as long as I found joy in the act of running. I couldn't go back and start my whole life over, but I could start my life over as a runner. In time, I would be a runner with only 30 extra kilos of weight ... then 25, 15, and 10. In time, I would be a runner who could run 50 metres, a mile, then a 5-K, and eventually a marathon.

It was being a runner that mattered, not how fast or how far I could run. The joy was in the act of running and in the journey, not in the destination. We have a better chance of seeing where we are when we stop trying to get somewhere else. We can enjoy every moment of movement, as long as where we are is as good as where we'd like to be. That's not to say that you need to be satisfied forever with where you are today. But you need to take pride in what you've accomplished, rather than thinking only of what's left to be done.

I should have known better. I should have been able to see the joy in the journey. It wasn't a new concept to me. I'd ridden thousands of miles on motorcycles. I didn't ride to get somewhere; I rode because I needed and wanted to ride. I loved to ride so much that a friend once told me I had 'white line fever'. Nothing in the world was as satisfying or as calming to me as watching the white line on the highway pass just

lessons learned

i'm dead last at a lot of races ... but won an award from my running club for racing over 250 miles in 2000! I wish I'd known earlier on that it was OK to be slow. Looking back, I've run off and on for years but never considered myself a runner because I couldn't run a 10-minute mile. I spent a lot of time struggling against my slowness rather than enjoying what I could do. After I finally realized that I was, after all, a runner, it gave me such confidence! I can now run over 13 miles at one time!

– Lisa White, aged 36
Running off and on for a few years
(but only with a 'runner's mindset' for the past 2)

below my feet. It didn't matter where I was going; it only mattered that I was moving. I wasn't heading anywhere in particular, but I was making good time.

I don't know if it was the movement or the sense of being in control that mattered most. My hand on the throttle determined my speed. The freedom came from knowing that, with a simple twist of my wrist, I could pass the car in front of me, and that I controlled the speed at which my world went by. It was the *act* of riding that mattered. The sights, sounds and smells of being on the road fed my spirit. Seeing my shadow racing along beside me stirred my soul. Knowing I was free to go where I wanted made me feel most completely alive.

Exploring the Wonders of Running

It may be difficult for those with greater talent to believe that those feelings are present now when I run. It's the same joy. When I run down a familiar path, it's like visiting an old friend. I feel the joy. When I discover a new route, it's the same joy as making a new friend. The joy is in the magic of the movement, in the elegant simplicity of passing by the world instead of watching while the world passes by you.

The joy is in knowing that I'm not stuck somewhere. I know that my feet and legs are strong enough to carry me away from where I am to somewhere I want to be. Running brings the knowledge that I am not bound by anything. I'm not bound by my past; I'm not bound by my present. The road is there ahead, inviting me to explore all the wonders that it holds.

Movement is the proof that I'm alive. Every step is confirmation of my place on the planet, of my ability to move through time and space. When I hear my heart pound and feel the air being sucked into my lungs, when I feel the heat, the cold, the baking sun, the pouring rain, I know that I am alive.

Because of running, I'm a little more alive every day. What was once a slow, steady march towards old age has become a race to cover all the miles my life will allow. Each step is one step further than I thought I would get and one step closer to where I'm going.

Those who wonder why you run and race won't always understand. They won't understand the joy of running in a spring rain or the sweat of satisfaction on a hot summer evening. They'll shake their heads as you put on your tights and vest to run in the autumn chill. They'll look at you as if you're crazy when you layer up to run on a snowy winter night.

But then, they won't see the field of wild flowers that you pass when you're running. They won't feel the cool mountain air. And they won't see the colours in the trees at an autumn marathon.

Those moments of joy will be yours to keep and yours to share with other runners. Those moments, more than how fast or how far you run, will distinguish you as a runner. Those moments as a runner will become the seams that hold together the fabric of your spirit.

Keeping Score

**Keep track instead of keeping score.
You'll discover that your worst – like your best –
lasts only an instant and that accepting your
limitations liberates you to become yourself**

Most of us are keeping score all the time. We compare our toys, incomes, educations and homes to those around us. Sometimes, the scorekeeping works out in our favour. But more often we choose to keep score with those against whom we can't compete. When that happens, tallying the score becomes an exercise in failure.

Keeping score is an irresistible temptation to adults. As a runner, the temptation to compare yourself to those around you is reinforced by the very nature of the sport. We wouldn't need a clock if who was running faster and slower didn't matter. If it was really just about the joy of it all, we wouldn't need to make sure we lined up with people who run at our speed. Keeping score is very difficult to avoid as a runner. You must compete in your age group, identify yourself by gender and quantify yourself before you even get to register for the race. Despite all the measures, you *can* stop keeping score and find joy in your own effort.

The need to keep score is burned deep into our psyches. I imagine the first words spoken in a human language were, 'Mine is bigger than yours.' It may have been in reference to a cave or a kill, but I'm willing to bet that the motivation to learn to speak began with one person wanting to tell another that he had more of something.

Contemporary culture not only supports this annoying behaviour of comparison, it encourages it. Keeping score of who has more of what is bad enough, but we take it a step further by telling each other when we have less as well as more. We've perfected the art of keeping score in reverse. Retailers of every description take pride in telling us that their prices are lower than their competition's and that they're making less profit. It's maddening.

This corruption-by-comparison starts early in life. We're compared to siblings or schoolmates. We're ranked by age, height, weight and intelligence. We're placed into per centiles before we can even begin to understand what it means. (I'm still not sure I understand!)

Runners aren't immune from this cultural behaviour. Nothing is more fun than listening to a group of highly skilled runners (or even some not so highly skilled) lying to each other about their training volume and pace. The conversation begins as a comparison of miles or speed and then turns into a death-defying foray into the unbelievable.

Experienced runners have perfected the art of keeping score of the more and the less comparisons. They run more miles, but in less time.

lessons learned

Be patient with yourself. Improvements will come with time. When I stopped training in late 1997, I was up to 20-mile runs. After, I was a slug for about 10 months. When I started running again in August of 1998, I literally couldn't run 10 minutes without walking. I wanted to cry. But I stuck with it, and the improvements that I knew would come did.

**– Ward Reed, aged 37
Running for 16 years**

The masters of the art of more and less are golfers. They actually brag about spending more money on clubs so that they can take fewer strokes with those very clubs.

Earlier in my life, I thought that this irrepressible hyperbole occurred only in motor sports. We called it bench racing. Mostly it was lying – about horsepower, top speed and what we had or hadn't done to the engine.

Runners have their own form of bench racing, but it's still lying. It's still inflating the numbers so your scorecard looks better than someone else's. For runners, it's about miles per week and pace per mile, but it's no different. It's a game you don't have to play to win.

Avoiding the Average

The one word we understand at a very young age is 'average'. We learn exactly what it means to be 'below average'. It isn't good. Even if we don't know what average is, we know that it's better to be above average than below. Unless, of course, it's better to be below average. We want a below average interest rate on our mortgages, a below average price for our cars, and below average cholesterol or resting heart rate. Anything, it seems, is better than average.

As we become adults, we're tempted to judge our worth only in relative terms. We forget how to look at our value in the absolute. We forget how to be content with ourselves as ourselves. We lose sight of how great it is to just be us. We think we need to keep score.

The power of the need to be 'above average' hit home in my previous job during a very heated discussion over merit pay increases. It was my job to defend the distribution of merit funds. I calmly explained that 50 per cent of the increases would, by definition, be below average. A colleague jumped to his feet and exclaimed: 'But here, we're all above average.' He was serious.

The problem for beginning runners and mature athletes is that the sport of running has a clear formula for assessing value. That isn't going to change. Running, as a sport, values speed. The formula is remarkable in its simplicity: how fast can you go over a given distance? The application of this formula is that the first runner across the finish line is the best and the last runner is the worst. If you measure only time over distance, you're forced to agree. So the traditionalists would have you believe that, but there are those of us who aren't quite ready to accept this measure of our worth.

However, there's still no hope for me, unless we start an 'Orpheus and Bacchus' category that's open only to former musicians who drank too much. Then, maybe an age group award would be in my future.

This constant scorekeeping robs us of our unique ability to be our best – not some arbitrary, historical or mathematical best. It's not easy to trust that your best is good enough. I'm sure you've been encouraged to do your best, when you *knew* there was a hidden message in the encouragement. Most of us knew that our best will be compared with someone else's best, and that ours will likely suffer by the comparison.

If we aren't careful, we begin to use our best as a weapon against those comparisons and standards. We throw up our hands when we fail and say, 'I gave it my best shot!' In response to someone else's disappointment in us, we defend ourselves by saying, 'It was the best I could do.' In those moments, our best is not enough, and we know it.

Keeping Track, Not Keeping Score

Running can teach us to define our best as our best instead of *the* best; not as the best of all time but just our best, and more important, as our best for today. Running can teach us to stop keeping score and start keeping track to move from comparison to compassion, and from competition to cooperation. Your best is not some static state. Your best is fluid and changing every day. And your best isn't always better than what it was. Sometimes, your best isn't even close to your 'best' best.

You learn to live with the gradual and dramatic shifts in your abilities as a runner. Your legs, lungs and heart are not factors that you can control, but rather elements that you must consider. You learn that the

an exercise in joy

A training log can help you see your successes. You can simply use a calendar, day planner or even a fancier 'training log' to record your workouts, chronicling your best you, not someone else's version of your best you as a runner. In addition to the typical distance, speed and type of workout, you also might jot down your mood and feelings. Today might not have been the fastest or furthest you've run, but was it the first time you ran and felt like a god or goddess? Was it the first time you noticed the sun sparkling off the leaves? Was it the first time you noticed the smell of your neighbour's drying sheets? Your moments of joy are just as important as your speed and distance.

most important skill is the ability to assess what your best can and will be at any given moment. You learn, too, that your best or anyone's best is really no more than a snapshot in your life.

When you stop keeping score, you discover that your worst, like your best, lasts only an instant. Your best and your worst occur in the here and now, and are then gone forever. Running can teach you how to let go of your worst moments while clinging to your best. If you can learn to accept how ephemeral your best is, you can accept the same about your worst. If you can accept that your best will pass you by very quickly, you can accept that your worst will pass by with the same speed. By giving up on keeping score, you can come to see both your best and worst as points on a map. They become mileposts in your journey. Nothing more.

Journal of a Journey

As contradictory as it sounds, I've found that the best way to stop keeping score is by keeping a training journal. A training journal will help you keep track instead of keeping score. This doesn't have to be an elaborate book with charts and graphs or a sophisticated computer program that spews out data in seven designer formats and six gorgeous colours. A training journal can be as simple as a small calendar.

My training journals, especially my early training journals, are a silent testimony to my drive, my will and my tenacity to change my life. They are the evidence of my transformation. Those journals record all the miles and times that I ran and walked. Those journals chronicle all the joys and sorrows of a person trying to re-create himself.

In many ways, I was lucky. When I first started, I didn't know anyone else who ran. This was, believe it or not, before the advent of the Internet, in the dark ages when we couldn't communicate instantly with anyone, anywhere. So I kept track of my runs in the naïve belief that I was making the same kind of progress that everyone else was.

My first training journals were nothing more than marks on the days of the week. I crossed off the days that I ran. Of course, I became obsessed with making the marks. An unmarked day stared back at me and taunted me. Crossing off the days became my 'mark of Zorro'.

As my training became more sophisticated, I found that I needed room in the journal to keep track of more than just the days I ran. I needed to record my mileage and pace, the weather conditions and how I felt before, during and after my run.

Eventually, I began keeping track of heart rates and running routes. I noted when I bought a new pair of shoes. I distinguished tempo runs from long, slow runs and differentiated between a training effort and a racing effort. I slowly began to see how complicated my running life had become.

I bought a computer-based training log that provided charts and graphs of my pace, time, distance, calories expended, running routes, mileage on my shoes and so on. I was able to compare my running weeks and months to each other. Eventually, I was able to retrieve and study more and more years of running data.

Each entry became it's own reward. I didn't have someone else's journal to examine and compare. Only my own. It was only my miles that counted, only *my* pace that mattered. Ultimately, it was only my running that made me a runner. And I had the proof right there in front of me in my training log.

It's your running that will make you a runner, too. It's your miles that matter most to you. It's finding the numbers that fit your life that will determine your success or failure as a runner. The miles that count are not the ones called for in a training programme or the ones that your running buddy ran.

lessons learned

The thing that I wish I had known before starting to run would be that the longer you run, the nicer people are to you!

– Doug Shearer, aged 63 Running all his life

The goal is to discover how to become the best runner you can be. If that means you have the potential to be a world-class athlete, then appreciate that gift and make the most of it. If, like me, your potential is simply to get out there and train and race with effort and enthusiasm, then prize that gift as well.

Having failed to do someone else's best is no criterion for failure. You and I can do no more than our best on any given day. We can't compete against a universal and arbitrary standard. If we accept this as runners, we must also accept it in other areas of our lives.

Learning not to keep score is one of running's most profound lessons. Learning to accept our own limitations, our own unique combinations of talent and will, our own exclusive coalitions of mind, body and spirit releases us to become ourselves. As a runner, you affirm these truths for yourself every day.

Mind Games

If your mind and body are always at odds, it's hard for either to feel good. Fire your inner critic and discover the truth: you're a winner!

A friend once asked me whose voice it was that I heard in my head when I was being critical of myself. Who was it that was telling me what I should be able to do? Who was it that was never satisfied with who I was and what I was becoming? It was a sobering question.

Is there a voice like that in your head? Does a little character sit on your shoulder all day long and evaluate your every move? Do you hear that voice berating your every mistake and belittling your every success? Many of us do. I believe nearly all of us do.

I had that voice, but for me, sadly, the voice was my own. I couldn't blame it on anyone else. I couldn't conjure up an image of a person or place that made me feel that way. By the time I was ready to start a life of activity, by the time I put on my running shoes and tried to change the direction of my life, I was the person who was the least cooperative.

Many of us berate ourselves and belittle our accomplishments in the misguided belief that it will encourage us to reach for a higher standard. Rather than using a positive voice to celebrate our success, we constantly undermine our progress by reminding ourselves how far we have to go. In the end, the constant criticism works to defeat us. We do this to ourselves all the time. How often have you heard someone chastising himself for a mistake? How often have you done it to yourself? Do you wonder to whom it is you're talking? Do you wonder who it is that's talking?

Inner Voices

I learned from a very good friend just how powerful that other voice can be. It was a lesson that I would have preferred not to learn at all, but we can't always choose who the teacher will be.

The lesson came at an earlier point in my life when I decided to lose weight and get fit. It was, as I recall, about the 300th time I had decided to get fitter and be more active. This time I had a better plan. This time, instead of just starving myself, I was going to starve myself and play squash.

I chose squash because the game was played in a confined area, so you never had to run very far chasing after errant balls. Since you could bounce the ball off every surface, aim and accuracy didn't seem to be as important. I learned too late that little things like speed and reaction time were important in squash. I had also tried playing tennis but spent all my time chasing after balls that I either missed completely or hit so hard they sailed into the next county. Looking back, I suppose it was good exercise, but it wasn't at all like the tennis playing I'd seen on television.

A friend, who was a former student athlete, took me under his wing (I really think he took pity on me) and agreed to teach me the fundamentals of squash. He demonstrated the art of the serve, talked about the flight of the ball and the angle of the racquet head, and amazed me with feats of backspin. Then he served the first ball to me and watched in utter terror as I swung wildly, missed the ball by at least 1 metre, and nearly severed his head with my racquet.

He decided that some individual practice might be better and outlined skill exercises for me. I worked diligently at serving. I practised hitting the ball with a forehand and a backhand. I bought goggles, a fancy racquet and even fancier shoes. Eventually, we tried playing a real game. Despite my efforts, he beat me easily for months.

Suddenly and without warning, I began to score a few points. We both were shocked. Much to my surprise and his chagrin, every now and then, I hit a good shot. At first, the ball just went in the general direction that I intended. Eventually, it went where I wanted it to go. The first time I put some backspin on the ball was like winning the lottery. My joy was unrestrained.

As I began to make a game of it, the game itself, which until then had been one of easy victory for him, took a decidedly negative turn. He was no longer able to have his way. He was no longer able to bolster his own ego by relishing how much greater his skill was than mine. Our relationship changed almost instantly from being teacher and pupil to being rivals and competitors.

I knew it had changed because he started yelling at the ball. Sometimes he yelled at the racquet. Sometimes he yelled at the wall or ceiling. Sometimes he even yelled at me. But mostly, he yelled at the ball. He told the ball how stupid it was when the shot didn't go where he thought it should go. He told the ball that it had no skill, that it wasn't trying hard enough, that it would never be any good.

lessons learned

Know where you are going! My first 'long run' was going to be 2 miles, 1 mile out and back. But because it was such a beautiful day, I went further and ended up lost and without fluid replenishment. Although I did get to meet a neighbour when I nearly passed out on his lawn while begging for water, I would much rather have presented myself in a more coherent state of mind!

**– M. J. Britton, aged 40
Running for 6 years (cancer survivor for 7)**

an exercise *in* joy

If you've ever trained a dog, then you know positive reinforcement motivates much more than negative criticism. If simply saying 'good boy' or 'good girl' taught your dog to sit, lie down, stay, come and heel, just imagine what similar positive words can do for your running. This week, pay attention to your self-talk before, during and after your runs. When you find yourself saying, 'But I need to get so much faster,' or 'Who was I to think I could be a runner,' try replacing those thoughts with something more positive, something that celebrates the numerous successes you've already achieved as a runner.

I laughed at first. Then I realized he wasn't yelling at the ball; he was yelling at himself. More important, I began to realize that he was the ball, and the voice was the voice of someone else who had yelled those very things at him. He – a talented, skilled, educated, professional person – still clung to the negative images of himself that someone else had provided.

The game stopped being fun for both of us. The court got crowded because there were at least three games going on at the same time. There was our real game, his mind game and my mind game.

My mind game was very different from his. If I even made contact with the ball, that is if I hit it intentionally and altered its flight, I squealed with satisfaction. This alone may have distracted him, but I was finding a childlike delight in the game. The pleasure came not so much in scoring points and beating him, but in scoring points and not beating myself.

The Mind-body Connection

Runners, it seems, are always running on at least two routes: the one beneath their feet and the one between their ears. It isn't often that these two routes are run simultaneously. Getting your feet and your mind in sync is much more difficult than most runners admit.

The training plan, for example, may call for an easy run. Your mind knows that. Your mind looks at the plan and the weather, decides on the shoes and shorts, and gets you out the door. But your mind isn't the only factor.

That may be the same day you realize 50 metres after you begin running that you woke up with someone else's legs. You have spring in your step, you're covering the ground faster than you've ever run before and you want to keep going. Your mind and your body need to talk.

It can go the other way just as often. Your training programme says today's workout should be a high-intensity or long-distance run. Your mind doesn't feel the fatigue in your legs or in your spirit. Your mind just sees the plan.

Those are the days when you realize in the first 50 metres that overnight you contracted some mystery disease that turned your legs into putty. Your mind is ready to run the plan, but your body isn't even ready to plan to run.

What you do on either of these days plays an important role in your life as a runner and in the satisfaction that you'll get from your running. If your mind and your body are always at odds about your running, it will be difficult for either to feel very good. If you're forever comparing the run you wanted to do or the run you were supposed to do with the run you did do, there will forever be conflict.

As often as runners are reminded to do so, we can't always listen just to our bodies. If I listened only to my body, I would stop running, grab a beer, light up a cigarette and never get off the sofa again. My body is not to be trusted when it comes to believing in the benefits of effort.

Neither is my mind. My mind can just as easily be tricked into thinking that I should be doing more or less. My mind can fall victim, as easily as my body, to thinking that I'm doing great or poorly, when neither is necessarily true. Like my body, my mind by itself can't be trusted.

As a runner, you'll have to find a means of communication between your mind and your body. You'll have to find a common ground and a language that both mind and body can speak. You need to have a system that allows each to overcome the other when it's appropriate.

A new runner approached me and told me she just couldn't run for more than 30 minutes. That was it, she said. She had tried, but because she couldn't run longer than that, she decided that she wasn't a runner and could never be one. My response was, 'Says who?'

Who says that someone who can't run more than 30 minutes isn't a runner? What voice inside that woman's head was telling her that? Who ordained that the magic time defining a runner is minutes? She had no answer. Her challenge wasn't in her body; her challenge was in her mind. It was the game in her mind that was the most difficult for her to win.

I asked her if she thought she could walk for 30 minutes. When she answered 'Yes,' I suggested that she start by alternating running 1 minute and then walking 1 minute for a total of 30 minutes. We needed to trick her mind. The voices in our heads don't give up easily. The voice in her head that told her she couldn't run more than 30 minutes wouldn't concede without a struggle. Instead of trying to convince that voice that it was wrong, she compromised. She allowed her mind to be right until her body realized it was wrong.

lessons learned

I wish I had known I should listen to my own body and myself. I underestimated how natural the act of walking and running is. In retrospect, I've never seen a toddler open a book on first steps.

– Sue Barmess (aka Sue Zooper), aged 47 Running for 14 years

Firing Your Inner Critic

Discovering your critical voice and identifying its source doesn't happen overnight. Sometimes it takes a dramatic event to uncover the true identity of your critic.

I discovered my inner critic somewhere on a back road during a distance triathlon. On that race morning, I stood in the lake ready to swim 1.25 miles, bike 56 miles, and then run 13.1 miles. I was prepared for the challenge, but not for the change that was about to take place in my life.

The swim went well. Sort of. I swam well enough, even though at one point I was swimming along the shoreline instead of towards it. I probably would have swum right round the lake instead of across it if the race volunteers hadn't stopped me.

Finding my bicycle was easy, since it was the only one left in the transition area. I took off on the bike at a dead sprint, trying to catch my friend Lee. About 10 miles into the bike portion, I caught up with him. He was crouching on the ground trying to help a female competitor mend a flat tyre.

Being the hard-core triathlete that I was, I stopped and helped him help her. Together we managed to change the tube and get the wheel back on the bike. We left her to inflate the tyre and hurried on our way. About 15 minutes later, she passed us like we were tied to a tree.

The first ominous sign of the day was the sun coming up and the clouds disappearing. Even on the bike, we could feel the heat of the road. The further we pedalled, the hotter it got and the more worried Lee began to look. Hours later, we arrived at the transition area to start the run.

As we left, we could see that the medical tent was already full. The day was beginning to take its toll on the participants. The searing heat and baked, black asphalt combined to make the run course a furnace. The out-and-back route gave us plenty of chances to see others heading back towards the finish line. Many of the competitors looked not like the walking wounded but like death itself. They were staggering, faces drawn and pale. They were hurting. Lee and I pressed on.

Somewhere near the turn-around, Lee slowed, barely walking, and urged me to go on at my own pace. Alone and moving in the direction of the finish line, I encountered nothing but my own thoughts. I was naïve about my own physical condition and unaware of my own state of dehydration. I moved forwards, feeling my shoes peel off the soft surface of the road with every step. I began to hallucinate.

At mile 10, I saw giant figures from my youth standing on the hillside. I saw my primary school teacher, who told me I'd never learn to spell. I saw my school band director holding the giant drumstick that he used as a baton. I saw them all, the faces and shapes of everyone in my life who had ever told me what I couldn't do.

One small voice whispered that I could stop now, and no one would know or care. After all, the voice continued, you're not an athlete anyway. No one will notice if you stop now. No one will care if you sit down and give up.

Those giant ghosts gathered on the road in front of me. I saw their leering faces, their laughing eyes. I felt their breath on me as I ran with all my might through their bellies. I was free of them. In that moment,

lessons learned

Over the years, I've learned to keep scanning the ground ahead for objects and potholes; that I can only increase my distance slowly; that if I wear a cotton garment in the rain, it will soak up the moisture and weigh me down; that lining up at the front of the pack and trying to race with the élites is not such a great idea for the average runner; that it's better to rest an injury than to tough it out; that winter running outdoors is not as bad as I thought it would be; that coaching from an experienced runner really does help; that I should always bring extra safety pins to a race; and of course, that running can be really enjoyable when you run with friends.

– Jonathan R. Zuckerman, aged 44
Running for 4 years

the voice changed. All the other voices fell silent and I could hear the faint sounds of encouragement.

As I crossed the finish line, I collapsed on the ground and just sat there. In the distance, I heard a child crying. It wasn't the sound of pain; it was the sound of agony. It was a deep anguish that had built up for years. I sat there listening to that child until one of the volunteers asked if I needed medical help. Only then did I realize that the crying, that voice, was coming from inside me. The only voice I'd ever heard was my own. I was the one telling myself what I could and couldn't do.

Whose voice do you hear inside your head? Whose voice narrates the tapes? Who is it that's the spokesperson for your soul? I discovered that it was my own voice. I had learned to speak the language of all my other critics, but the voice was mine. Running can help us change that voice, from being our worst critic to being our biggest fan. Running can help us see that it's rarely our bodies that hold us back; it's our minds.

Running is the road to self-acceptance. Our feet can teach our minds that we are only what we are. Our feet can teach our minds to congratulate us and to celebrate our strength in pursuing our dream. If we listen closely enough, at every pace and every distance, we can hear that voice telling us that we are runners and that we are winners.

Playing to Win

You may never win a race, but the years ahead can be filled with victory after victory

Make no mistake: winning is better than losing. But feeling that you've given your all in the pursuit of a personal goal is more satisfying than a hollow victory. Putting all of the pieces together – training plan, race strategy, mental toughness and physical effort – results in an unmatched sense of well-being and contentedness.

It's also the best allegory for living life to its fullest. Life can't be taken so seriously that you live it without risk. There are times in life, as in running and racing, when the only way to see tomorrow is to walk right up to the edge of today.

Other runners are surprised by how competitive I am. No one likes to be passed by 'The Penguin' in races, so I often find myself in a battle to the death with someone I've never met. I suppose I ought to give in to their need to beat me, but I can't.

Runners nearer the front erroneously assume that those at the back are just out for an organized group jog with water stops. Nothing could be further from the truth. When I put on a race number, I'm there to race. If that race happens to occur between me and a 75-year-old woman or a 12-year-old boy, so be it. They're going to have to find a way past me. I'm not going to willingly yield. If challenged, I'll reach down to summon all the energy I have left and put it all on the line, even if, as in one marathon, I'm competing for 15,342nd place. I didn't want to finish in 15,343rd place without giving it my best shot!

The difference, I hope, is in perspective. There may be a big differential in the prize money between 1st place and 10th place in a major marathon, but the medal is the same whether you're 15,342nd or 15,343rd. Those at the back of the pack know it. Despite the furiousness of our competition, we also know that, in the end, it matters only to us.

This perspective doesn't mean turning away from competition. It doesn't mean we can't fight tooth and nail for our place in the finishing order or that there's never a time when losing doesn't haunt us. But it means we accept that winning and losing are equally important.

Personal Victories: They Really Matter

In the past, I didn't understand the drive to be competitive if you clearly weren't going to win. I watched motor sports races and I didn't care if there was a great battle going on for 25th place. I wanted to see the leader. I wanted to see how and when he won. I didn't care if he was leading by 10 laps over the rest of the field. It was watching a winner that kept me interested.

Years ago, I witnessed an incident so disturbing that I was unable to put it in perspective at the time. I wasn't ready to learn this particular lesson until I began to run and compete.

I had gone with friends to watch a motorcycle road race at a small road course. The point of the day was to ride our own motorcycles to the race and back. We hung around and watched the races for most of the afternoon. This wasn't a high-level, national class race competition. It was primarily young men trying to make their mark in motorcycle racing or old guys who finally had enough time and money to play 'boy racer'. The course was a narrow strip of poorly maintained asphalt that meandered through trees and fields.

Motorcycle races are organized by class, usually engine size and then by experience. Unlike running, a neophyte motorcycle racer cannot line up with the best in the world. A rider moves up in the professional echelons by winning races. So even in the lowest classes, the competition is fierce.

We watched an endless stream of modestly talented young riders flailing their way around the beat-up track. It was getting late and we decided to sit on the hillside near the last turn to be closer to the action where we knew most of the battles for position would occur.

Time after time the riders came past, motorcycles banging together as they fought for the inside or the outside line or any line at all. They were forced off the asphalt into the grass, slid harmlessly to a stop, picked up their bikes, and got back onto the track. So we thought nothing of it when we saw the young rider fall as he battled for a meaningless position at the back of the pack. As he sat up, surprised to find himself off his bike and facing the oncoming riders, it was clear he wasn't upset about crashing. He just wanted to get back in the race.

In a split second, another young rider who was probably as inexperienced as the rider on the ground, came around the curve and rode full speed into the fallen racer. The front wheel of the oncoming motorcycle hit the young rider in the stomach and chest and literally rode over the top of him with both wheels. I had never seen anyone die before. I'd never seen the life leave a body. As he lay there on the track, we knew. There was no mistaking the presence of death.

For years, I wondered what made someone fight so hard for something so meaningless. What made someone risk his life for something that didn't matter? I didn't understand why a young man would be willing to die for 24th place.

The day I lined up for my first race, I understood. I understood as I pinned on my race number and felt the primal urge inside me come to life for the first time in my life. I understood that there was less difference between that young man and me than I had thought.

an **exercise** *in* **joy**

How are you victorious? How are you a winner? During your next run or race, think about what demon you are battling and what victory you are running towards. Chronicle these victories in your running log. You may be surprised to learn that the same victory you reach through running is a metaphor for your daily life.

Wins and Victories

The emphasis on winning and the attitude that second place is the first loser misses the point of the sport of running. That attitude demeans the efforts of those who lose as well as those who win. It prevents all of us, as runners, from appreciating and participating in each of our victories. There's a difference between a win and a victory, between winning and being victorious, and between being a winner and being a victor.

To win is to accept the rules of the contest, the standards of the sport and the conditions set forth by the conventions of the game, and then doing more or less of whatever is quantified to determine the winner. That may be the most points, least strokes or shortest time from start to finish. A win happens only in that moment and in relative terms. You can't have a winner without a loser.

In any race, there will be an overall winner, someone who crosses the finish line first. That person deserves the right to be called the winner, but that win isn't the only victory on the course on that day.

The difference between a win and a victory is another lesson that running can teach us, if we're willing to learn. We can learn it in our first 5-K or our 50th marathon. We can also spend years running and miss learning this lesson. If we're so focused on winning, so intent on finding someone outside of ourselves against whom we need to compete, losing will become not only a habit, but also a way of life.

The need to rise to meet a challenge is one of our greatest strengths. The need to reach down inside ourselves, to fight for 24th position or sprint the final 25 metres, is an essential weapon in our running arsenal. With practice and with awareness, the need to meet the challenge can be harnessed to serve our greatest need. That need, in almost every case, is getting to know who we are.

Testing Your Limits

We often underestimate our ability to be victorious. We decide before the battle begins that we don't have the skill to win, so we don't bother trying. Why bother to fight if you know you're going to lose?

The answer beat in the heart of that young motorcycle racer. It beats in the heart of the cancer survivor who walks a 5-K. The answer beats in the heart of the mother who lost a child and the son who lost his father and runs a marathon in their memory. The answer beats in your heart right now.

We want to know who we are. We want to know what our limits are. To live life in peace, we have to know how far we can go. As a runner, you need do nothing more than have a pair of shoes and a place to run in order to find those answers.

You may never have a chance to win a race, but you'll have ample opportunities to be victorious. You have years ahead of you that can be filled with victory after victory. Those victories can start on your first day as a runner and continue for the rest of your life.

I have never won a race. In fact, I've never even seen anyone win a race that I was running. I'm so far back that in some marathons the awards ceremony is over before I finish. The year Khalid Khannouchi set the world record, I was there, running on the same course. The difference was that he finished before I reached mile 11.

I've never won, but I've been victorious a thousand times. I've been victorious over my fear, my doubts, my own history, and over my need to make someone else a loser in order to feel like I've won. I've been victorious over my need to win every one of life's small battles. And I've been victorious over feeling like a loser in battles that I can't win.

But the will to be victorious is of no use to us if we don't know what battle we're fighting. Runners fear the course, the competition or the distance when the real enemy is the demons in our souls that conspire to snatch defeat from the jaws of victory. The willingness to prepare to be victorious is useless if we prepare for the wrong opponent.

While standing at the starting line, I don't think of the other runners as competitors. I don't see them as runners who are going to prevent me from winning. I see them as the very people who are going to help me be victorious.

I have led pacing groups with hundreds of people who are all working together towards the same goal. I've watched total strangers become best of friends in the pursuit of their dreams. I've watched two people share the joy of each other's victory long after the winner has gone home.

lessons learned

I wish I had known to be proud of my race finishing times, even though I was slower than almost everyone else. I spent too many years being embarrassed to tell others I ran 35-minute 5-Ks. I even found myself once trying to hide my 8-K time from other runners. Now I realize that the time on the clock is not a reflection of the kind of runner that I am. It is merely the time it took to cover that distance on that day. No more, no less. Today, I'm proud to tell anyone my race times, slow or not.

– Kecia LeCausi, aged 38
Running for 8 years

Sharing Your Victories

One of the most powerful moments in my life came in sharing someone else's victory. I was pacing the first half of a marathon. A young man stayed with me step for step for 13 miles. I relinquished the pacing to a friend at the halfway point and went to the finish line to wait.

At mile 26, I joined that same young man and we ran across the finish line together. As he crossed the line, his emotions exploded and he began to cry. I remembered my own tears when I finished my first marathon and went to him. We stood just behind the finish banner. He cried and I stroked his head – a young man and an ageing one in a scene as old as time. At that moment, he needed someone with whom he could share his victory. He needed someone to tell him that he was victorious.

I don't expect to see that young man again. Our lives crossed for that instant only. Yet, I learned from him the same lesson I learned from the young rider. The victories over ourselves are the ones that matter the most.

A Lesson for Life

Running has taught me that the very definition of victory is elusive. As in life, the challenges we face as runners keep changing. Our lives as runners and the lessons learned become inseparable from the rest of our lives. We learn that the greatest teacher we will ever find is already inside us.

Our victories in running become our victories in life. In the first stages of running, when improvement comes easily, the victory may be as simple as completing the first mile. Being victorious then is largely a matter of overcoming the inertia that binds us to our past selves.

In the middle age of our running lives, victories have much more drama. Other characters appear in our play. Becoming a victor involves more than going beyond our expectations. A victory at this stage requires going beyond our imaginations. Being victorious over the battle against our past gives way to being victorious over the battle against our future.

During the sunset years of our running and our lives, victory is about letting go – of how we used to be and of what we thought we would be. Being a victor means making peace with how far we've come, yet how little progress we've made.

The miles that we've run are our most loyal companions and our most trusted friends. Morning runs when the sun touches the dew on green grass deepen our appreciation for how simple joy can be. Evening runs when the sun dips below the horizon and casts the world in shades of red remind us of the passing of time in our lives.

It is through the act of running that we become runners. It is running that gives us a runner's heart, a runner's mind and a runner's soul. That most of us will never feel the thrill of winning is no excuse to abandon the search for our own personal victories.

The spirit that drives the mature athlete is buried deep inside. Trophies and ribbons don't fuel it. It's nourished by the relentless need to find that as-yet-untapped source of energy and enthusiasm within ourselves. It is knowing that we have both accepted and rejected the limitations of our running and of our lives that makes all of us winners.

lessons learned

If you are one of those millions of runners who's slow, I mean really slow, it's all right. Do not try to keep up with other runners. Do not worry about looking dumb. Most of the other runners have been there in one form or another, and the ones who haven't are all up in front and can't see you anyway.

**– Sarah Kendall, aged 19
Running for 2 years**

Basic Truths about
Racing

Let's race! Everything you need to know about running's ultimate joy – from training to the post-race party

In my wilder and, some might say, misspent youth, I was involved in many kinds of motor sport racing. When the risks of drag racing on the street became too high, I sought out more legitimate racing venues. It didn't matter to me what kind of racing it was. I tried everything from autocross to trials riding, from rallying to motorcycle dirt-track racing. I just wanted to be a racer.

In those days, most racing actually took place in the garage. A group of very earnest young men would gather to discuss the finer points of balancing connecting rods, polishing intake manifolds and the wisdom of shaving weight off critical frame parts. We drank a lot of beer, smoked a lot more cigarettes and dreamed about what it would be like to be a racer.

In one weak moment, I found myself a partner on a grand prix motorcycle sidecar race team. You don't see sidecar racing much because of all the international racing classes sidecars are clearly the stupidest. In brief, sidecar racing involves bolting a platform and outboard wheel onto a motorcycle, then convincing someone to throw his weight back and forth to make the thing go faster in the turns.

The person who moves left and right over the back of the motorcycle and platform at speeds in excess of 120 mph is called the monkey. I was the monkey. Good monkeys have three essential qualities. They are agile, fearless and *really* stupid. I was just stupid, but I was a racer.

My motorcycle racing career ended moments after I lost my grip in a fast, sweeping curve and skipped along the racetrack like a flat stone on a calm lake. I still remember the sound of my helmet striking the asphalt and wondering how far I would slide and bounce before I hit something very hard. I still remember wondering if the riders behind me would be able to avoid hitting me.

I explain all this as a way of helping you understand that racing is one of the best ways of building and preserving the joy of running. It's racing – lining up with a number pinned on your chest – that makes it all worth it. And, of course, wandering around the shopping centre in a race T-shirt is about the biggest kick in the world.

You see, no one in the shopping centre knows where you finished. No one knows whether you were first or last. It doesn't make any difference. It doesn't make any difference while the race is going on, and it *sure* doesn't make any difference once the race is over. What matters is preparing for and participating in the ultimate in the running world – the race!

Some new runners are put off by the idea of racing because they think it's just for the fastest runners. The front of the pack in races *is* for the fastest runners, but in the middle of the pack – at any race, at any distance – you'll find yourself surrounded by runners like yourself. You'll find yourself competing for place and position and having more fun than you ever imagined.

Running versus Training

When you move from runner to racer, you also move from running to training. Everything changes when you become a racer. Your goals, the structure of your training, the risks and the rewards of your running life change dramatically the instant you fill out your first race application.

Your goals as a runner can be very undefined. You may want to run three days a week, or every day, or run 25 miles a week. To be a runner, you don't need much structure. You can simply lace up your shoes and run as far and as fast as you want every time you run. It doesn't take anything more complicated than that to be a runner.

As a racer, your goals become much more specific. You decide, for example, that you want to run a particular 5-K on April 20th. More specifically, your goal may be to run the race in a certain time. More specifically yet, your goal may be to run every mile faster than the previous. Once you've set such goals, you've accepted the risk of failing to meet them.

Your running life changes when you become a racer with race goals. As a racer, your training becomes much more structured. You calculate the number of months, weeks and days until the race. You work out how many of those days you can use for speedwork, endurance runs or threshold runs. Even your daily runs become much more structured. You know before you put on your shoes what that day's run is supposed to be.

Your risks change. Running, as a lifestyle, doesn't have many risks. There's not a lot of inherent danger in putting on the old running shoes and heading out of the door. But as a racer in training, the risks can be pretty serious. When you're training to race, you're always searching for your physical edge, always trying to find your limit. You push the envelope, trying to do as much as you can without getting injured. This is true whether you're training to break 30 minutes in a 5-K or 30 minutes in a 10-K. The process is the same.

It's the difference in the rewards that I enjoy the most. Running has its own rewards – stress reduction, a higher level of fitness, the camaraderie of other runners, beautiful scenery, the joy of the movement. These are important rewards, not to be taken lightly. The rewards of racing are much more immediate – the possibility of a PR (personal record), the chance to race a new distance, the opportunity to beat a runner who's always been ahead of you, the victory of helping another runner finish that last fatiguing mile!

> **lessons learned**
>
> *Volunteer for at least one race a year. Giving back to the running community is a great way to keep your running desire alive. Next time you pass a water station in a race, you'll be sure to thank those volunteers.*
>
> **– David Gegear, aged 30**
> **Running for 4 years**

In racing, you get to take your best effort – in planning, training and running – and put it up against someone else's best effort. You line up with racers like yourself who are no more certain of what kind of race they'll have than you are. You line up knowing that you're willing to put it all on the line. You're willing to find out who and what you are made of.

You'll find that racing is mostly about putting forth an honest effort. Far from the 'win at all costs' mentality, you'll find that runners are far more likely to celebrate your all-out effort at any speed or distance than to maintain a 'win at all costs' attitude. Once that number is pinned on, you're a racer just like every other élite or back-of-the-pack runner.

Off to the Races

I receive hundreds of e-mail questions a week from new runners. Most are the typical 'How many miles a week should I run?' or 'How can I get faster?' These questions are fun to answer. Once in a while, though, I receive an e-mail from someone who says, 'I've been running for three weeks and I want to do a marathon. Which one do you recommend?' These are difficult to answer because, although I admire the person's enthusiasm, I doubt their wisdom.

A local 5-K is the best place to start for almost all new runners. You can usually find information and applications for these races at your local running specialist store, gym or fitness centre. The alternative to the small local race is a giant national 5-K. Your goal should be the same in either case: show up prepared to have fun. It's also a good idea to convince a friend or family member to go to the race with you. You'll have someone to talk to on the way to the race and someone to brag to on the way home.

My friends are still amused by the story of my first race. Coming from a motor sports background, I had no idea what the protocol was at road races. I assumed there would be some kind of qualifying and that you would line up at the start in some predetermined order. Imagine my delight when I discovered you could line up wherever you wanted *and* that I would only be competing against old guys like me. I could barely contain myself. I lined up in the *front* row despite the fact that the fastest mile I'd ever run was a 10:30. (The leaders in my age group were running closer to 6-minute miles.)

Fortunately, a friend grabbed me and dragged me to the back of the pack. In fact, he dragged me to the very last row. I protested that we were giving up much too much ground to the leaders. I *knew* how fast I'd become (after all, my first miles were in the 18- to 20-minute range), and I felt like I had conceded victory by starting last. Starting last was a good thing. I finished last, too.

A Sample Training Programme

Great races almost always come down to great planning. A well-known quote is attributed to several people, but the message is the same: 'The will to win is meaningless without the will to prepare to win.' We're not out to win very many races, but our preparation needs to be just as disciplined.

In the weeks prior to a race, you can begin to assess your running strengths and weaknesses. You can do this without worrying about becoming self-critical and self-defeating. As a racer, you want and *need* to look honestly at what you do well and what you don't do well. Your training plan has to take into account the good and the not so good.

A sample 5-K training plan for the new runner, assuming four daily runs per week, might look something like this:

Day 1: Steady-state stamina run, approximately 35 per cent of your weekly mileage.

This is the *long* run that will strengthen your muscles and your mind. The key to this run is that it is the *long-slow* run. It should be at least 1 minute per mile *slower* than your daily run pace and up to 2 miles per minute slower than your 5-K–race goal pace.

Day 2: Speed play (fartlek), approximately 25 per cent of your weekly mileage.

This is a fun run. Warm up for about one-quarter of the total time you expect to run that day. Then start putting some 'pickups' into the run. These pickups don't have to be very long (between telegraph poles or postboxes), but they should be long enough that you feel like you've exerted yourself a little.

Do a pickup, then slow down and run easy for a few minutes, then do another pickup. Alternate the slow pace and pickup intervals until you've run about three-quarters of the total time, then run easy and cool down for the remaining quarter of the time.

Day 3: Speedwork, *no more* than 15 per cent of your total weekly mileage.

Speedwork takes many forms. The easiest to monitor is on a track. For 5-K training, focus your speedwork on quarter-mile (or 400 metres, i.e., one lap of a standard track) repeats.

After you've warmed up for a ½-mile, run one lap at the fastest speed that you can *sustain* for the entire lap. Bolting out fast and fading is not good. Find a pace you can run for the full lap. Rest an amount of time *equal* to the time it took you to run the lap, then run another. Start with four repeats or intervals and add one per week, up to 10 repeats.

Speed doesn't come just from effort. It comes from efficiency too. You can only push yourself so hard for so long. You can only do so much with your genetic potential. But you can become an efficient runner. Pay attention to how you are running. Are your arms pumping forwards and back or side-to-side? Is your breathing regular or is it out of control? You don't need to know very much about running to be able to see and hear when your form and efficiency improves.

Day 4: Easy recovery run, 25 per cent of your weekly mileage.

This run is exactly what it says it is: an *easy* recovery run. The pace of the recovery run may change from week to week. Listen to your

lessons learned

It's important to go out at a conservative, realistic pace in a race. My first distance race was a cross-country race. I sprinted to the front, stayed in the lead for a couple minutes, then had to stop and ended up throwing up behind a tree and walking back to the start.

– Howard White,
aged 43
Running for 31 years

body and be prepared at any point to cut the run short if that's what's best.

This is a *very* generic programme. It's designed to give you a sense of how you need to prepare. For a more detailed training programme, go to your local library or bookshop, or look online. Many 5-K training plans are available at *www.runnersworld.co.uk* and *www.ausrun.com.au*.

Before the Race

Many runners taper their training for longer races such as the half-marathon and marathon. This means that during the weeks leading up to the big day, they reduce their overall mileage to give their bodies and legs rest and a chance to repair any nicks and dents inflicted during the training.

You won't need to taper or back off your training very much leading up to a 5-K, but you should give your body and your mind time to feel fully refreshed and recovered from the strain of training. During the week preceding your 5-K debut, reduce your mileage by about 50 per cent, and back off the intensity by nearly 100 per cent. You won't help yourself by training hard the week before the race, and you can lose any chance of a good race by overdoing it.

The Night Before

A friend and coach recommends that you get completely dressed in your race clothes the night before the race. Take the clothes off and set them on a chair in the order you took them off. Then, in the morning, you can just step right back into your clothes.

I've saved myself countless sleepless nights and panicked mornings with this strategy. Pinning my number (on the *front*) before I go to bed helps get my mind into the warrior mode I'll need in the morning. If the number has a tear-off strip along the bottom, be careful not to pin that part to your shirt. The lower portion is often torn off at the finish for timing records.

Race Morning

If you slept at all (don't worry if you didn't), get up and get moving. For morning races, I eat a normal breakfast, but about half the amount I would normally eat. You don't want to show up at the starting line stuffed, but you don't want to be starving either. Avoid high fibre foods

Inspirational
Tools of the Trade

You've done it. You've completed the beginner's programme. You now have the tools you need to run joyfully for the rest of your life. You might run fast. Or, like me, you might waddle slowly. Or somewhere in between. Just remember that this is a journey. At times during your journey, you'll feel inspired, and at other times, you'll only notice the perspiration. Still other times, you'll feel dedicated. And finally, sometimes running will feel like one huge celebration.

To ensure that you experience your share of joyful moments, take the final step in your life as a beginning runner by signing up for your first 5-K. I promise you won't regret it. Look for a fun run or a charity race in your area to start, and then branch out from there. Before you know it, you'll be a regular on the racing circuit.

(such as porridge) that might encourage you to make a pit stop during the race.

Near the start line, almost all races will have some kind of facilities, ranging from a line of portable toilets to the boys and girls loos at the local junior school. But as best you can, try to get as much of the toilet business out of the way before you get to the race site. No matter how many portable toilets the race provides, there are never enough, and the queues are always long. (Just in case, it's always a good idea to stash some toilet paper in the pocket of your running shorts.)

I like to get to the site early. Sometimes it's the only way I'll ever see the finish line area all set up. By the time I finish, the entire finish line area is often dismantled and the clock is sitting on a metal folding chair.

The other reason to get there early, especially if it's your first race, is to meet new friends. Don't worry about being a novice. Every runner there was a novice at some point. Watch what people do, ask questions if you're unsure, and be prepared to have fun.

The Starting Line

A friend and colleague, Freddi Carlip, has developed an alter ego she calls Miss Road Manners. I've been on panels with Freddi, aka Miss Road Manners, and have seen her decked out in running shoes and elbow-length white gloves for the role. Freddi has developed guidelines for racing called the Rules of the Road; I've paraphrased some examples.

The starting line area of nearly every race can be divided into four categories. There are the runners who think they *can* win. They're standing right on the start line. There are the runners who think they *might* win. They're standing right behind the front row. There are the 'age-groupers', people from age 18 to 80 who know they can't win overall, but are pretty sure they can beat everyone in their age group. They're the middle 50 per cent of most race packs.

Then there are the Penguins. We used to be called 'back of the packers', as if we were content to be following behind the rest of the pack. Most of us aren't content. We're simply trying to find our place in the pack. The place to start is at the back.

Look around, ask around, and try to find a place where the runners near you have the same goals. If you're hoping just to finish, find a place squarely at the back. If you're thinking about trying to break 30 minutes or so, move up a bit. If you're trying to break 15 minutes, you're reading the wrong book.

When the runners are called to the start line, go. Say your goodbyes, put on your game face and line up. Pay attention to the pre-race instructions. They'll not only help you avoid a major mistake, they'll also help you get your mind focused on the racecourse ahead of you.

A Miss Road Manners tip: if you drop something as the race starts, either leave it or move to the side of the road and wait for the entire pack to pass. There's nothing quite as embarrassing as bending over and having 12 people run into you.

Things happen early in a race that may surprise you. In one of my first 5-Ks, someone stepped on my heel. The next thing I knew my shoe was sailing over my head. I watched in terror as it landed 15 metres ahead of me. A helpful soul scooped it up and tossed it backwards over his head – and over mine. Then it was 15 metres behind me. I went back, retrieved my shoe, pulled it on, and ran my 5-K personal record.

Off and Running

If you've gone to the race with friends, be careful to respect the right of the runners behind you and never, ever run or walk more than two abreast. Even if you think you're way at the back and no one could possibly care, you should still give all the runners their right-of-way on the course.

When you get to the water tables, slow down and grab a cup from a volunteer, but keep moving. Once you're clear of the water tables, you can move to the edge of the road and drink at your leisure. I tell you this because I used to approach the water tables like they were a buffet and stop to drink.

The exception to this rule is if you race in Florence, Italy. During the marathon there, volunteers fully expect those of us further back to stop and sample the food and drink. As one course worker said to me as I rushed away, 'Take your time; Florence will wait.'

If you hear someone coming up behind you, move to the right, or to the outside of the course if you have to, and let him or her pass.

If they yell something like 'on your left' or 'coming through' or 'excuse me,' try to signal them somehow so they know you've heard them.

If you need to stop, move off the racecourse if possible. Make sure that the runners around you know you're planning to stop. Wave your arms, shout your intention and then move over.

lessons learned

There can be a big difference between different running events. I was really lucky in that the first one I entered was a 5-K fun run, which was perfect for first-timers. Lots of walkers. The next two or three I entered were more in the genre of competitive 5-K races – big difference! If you're worried about speed, or would be disheartened by being at the back of the pack, make sure you pick a fun run or similar event, rather than a very competitive race. With so many events having the previous year's results online now, it's pretty easy to scope it out before registering.

– Amy Stanton, aged 34
Running for 3 years

The Finish Line

There it is – the finish line. You've *done* it! You've finished your first race. You can feel the adrenaline kick in. You can feel the temptation to run to the finish as fast as you can. You feel like a child again. It's fantastic.

Keep in mind that all the runners around you are feeling the same way, which means that you're surrounded by a bunch of emotionally charged people who are all on the verge of laughing or crying. Stay aware of what's going on around you.

Only registered runners should ever cross the finish line. If a well-meaning friend or relative has joined you for the last few hundred metres of the race, ask them to get off the course *before* you cross the finish line. It messes up the race results if unregistered runners cross the line, and besides, this is *your* moment. Savour it!

When you actually cross the finish line, don't stop. Keep moving through the finish line area. You may want to kneel down and kiss the ground at that point, but if you're not last, there are others behind you who are finishing, too. If you *are* last, you don't want to do anything to delay the volunteers from going home.

Most events have some kind of post-race refreshments. It took me a while to figure this out because I finished so late that all the food was usually gone. Keep in mind that there are other runners behind you (and faster runners who are out on their cooldown) who also need to eat.

After the Party's Over

For some runners, a race is like a final exam. They do all the planning and preparation and then show up on race morning to take the test. They even give themselves a score.

For other runners, runners like us, the race is the celebration. It's a celebration of the planning and the preparation. We show up on race morning like we're going to a party. We know that we'll be with people who share our dreams, goals and values. We know that there's no place on earth where we feel more at home than in a group of runners before a race.

We know that they're just like us. We know that they're ordinary people leading ordinary lives. We know that they have no more talent or discipline than we do. We know that they want from themselves what we want from ourselves – a chance to do our best.

When it's over, that's the only question any of us need ask. Did we do our best? Did we line up prepared to do our best, however we defined 'best' that day? One day, our 'best' may mean running as hard and as fast as we can. Another day, our 'best' may mean running slowly with a friend who needs encouragement. On still another day, our 'best' may mean simply savouring the experience of the run.

All of those things can be our best. Races are the best place to find the best of ourselves, the best of others, and the best of running.

Recommended Reading

▶ Benson, Roy. *The Runner's Coach*. Medway, OH: Cedarwinds Publishing, 1994.

▶ Burfoot, Amby. *The Runner's Guide to the Meaning of Life: What 35 Years of Running Has Taught Me about Winning, Losing, Happiness, Humility, and the Human Heart*. Emmaus, PA: Rodale Inc., 2000.

▶ Daniels, Jack. *Daniels' Running Formula: Programmes and Strategies: 1,500 to Marathon*. Champaign, IL: Human Kinetics, 1998.

▶ Higdon, Hal. *Run Fast: How to Train for a 5-K or 10-K Race*. Emmaus, PA: Rodale Inc., 1992.

▶ Noakes, Tim. *Lore of Running: Discover the Science and Spirit of Running.* 3rd edition. Champaign, IL: Human Kinetics, 1991.

▶ Sheehan, George. *George Sheehan on Running to Win: How to Achieve the Physical, Mental & Spiritual Victories of Running.* Emmaus, PA: Rodale Inc., 1994.

Afterword

Standing at the starting line of a marathon, your goal is to complete the 26.2 miles. As the marathon continues, that goal keeps changing. Eventually, your goal is to take that one final step across the finish line. The difference between succeeding and failing in our lives is often as simple as taking that one step.

For many of us, it isn't that last step of a marathon that matters most; it's the first step we take on our journey to becoming runners. The truth is that every step is important. Every step takes us a little closer to where we want to be. Every step frees us from a life of sedentary confinement. Every step uncovers some new possibility.

My hope is that you will have found something in this book that will help you find your own path to the joy of running. My dream is that you will find, as I did, that in our lives as runners, there is no finish line.

Waddle on, friends.

John 'The Penguin' Bingham

Special Bonus Section

My Greatest Hits

As a former music professor and musician, I can't resist the urge to slip musical references into my writing. This is one of those times.

At some point in their lives, most great musicians compile a 'greatest hits' album. Some compile many. I've been writing a monthly column in *Runner's World* magazine for such a long time that I simply couldn't resist the urge to compile my own 'greatest hits'.

The following columns are the most popular ones I've written, according to the amount of fan mail they generated. I hope you enjoy them as much as *Runner's World* readers did when they were first published.

Number One

May 1996

Looking up, I see the finish banner and clock. I pick up the pace, releasing the energy I've been saving for the final kick. I am gasping for air; my heart is pounding. I am going to have a PR. I am going to break 30 minutes for 5-K. What?

John Lennon may have been the Walrus, but I am the Penguin. I am the runner you've seen whose legs look as if they are tied together at the knees. I am the runner whose stride is the same as his shoe length. And I am not alone.

Why a penguin? Because metaphors usually used to describe runners – fleet-footed gazelles, cheetahs and winged-footed Mercury – don't have much to do with my running style. I tend to resemble a penguin waddling across the frozen tundra more than a thoroughbred in the homestretch.

If you've seen a penguin run or walk, you know what I mean. Penguins walk as if their feet are killing them. Penguins, waddling and scurrying, are the ultimate expression of will over form. Their feet move as fast as possible, but their bodies are barely propelled forwards at all.

Those of you who are gifted runners have seen penguin runners at races. Well, you've seen us at the races where the course is out and back. You rarely see us finish, however. We're the ones who are finishing as you are getting in your cars to go home.

Actually, penguins are easy to spot. We keep moving further and further away from the starting line before the race begins. As the really fast and pretty fast runners complete their pre-race warm-ups and position themselves for the perfect starting spot, we penguins keep getting pushed back. In small races we can still see the starting line, but in bigger races we're so far back we almost need a water station *before* the starting line.

Once the gun goes off, as the cheetahs and gazelles speed away from us in search of PRs and age-group awards, the penguins settle into the middle of the back of the pack. It's then, when we finally have the course to ourselves, that the real race for the penguins begins – the race with our fears and insecurities. We are not racing anyone but ourselves. In many cases we are not running *to* anything, but away from everything.

My running shoes have become giant erasers on my feet. Every foot strike rubs away some memory of a previous indiscretion with food or smoke or drink. Every successful mile releases me from the grip of the demons of failure. Every starting line is another chance to prove that my past will not determine my future.

When I am running, in training or in a race, I imagine myself as strong and swift and elegant. When I am running, I imagine myself striding gracefully through life with courage and pride. When I am running, I forget my failures as a child or parent or friend or lover. Through running, I create myself as I have always wanted to be.

And I have discovered that I am not alone. As I have admitted my own fears and hopes, I've discovered that many in the running community share those fears and hopes. We, the webbed-footed wonders, are about to come into our own.

And we will run to undo the damage we've done to body and spirit. We will run to find some part of ourselves yet undiscovered. Together, we will continue our odyssey of affirmation.

Waddle on, friends.

Becoming a Runner

February 1997

I'm not sure when it happened, but at some point I stopped being a person who simply ran and became a runner. It's not that something dramatic occurred. I am still out there waddling through the miles. I am still racing against the clock, which for me often means trying to finish before the clock is taken down.

No, the change was much more subtle. The act of running became less something that I did and more something that I was. I recently began to look at my life to see if I could find out what had changed.

Maybe the change was in my shoes. I have, by actual count, 26 pairs of running shoes in various stages of decay. So the oldest have been retired to a sacred spot in the cupboard; the newest sit in a pile at the foot of the bed, like so many puppies waiting to be played with.

But how can I throw out the shoes in which I ran my first 5-K or my first marathon, or the racing flats I bought to reward myself for my first sub-10–minute mile?

Maybe the change happened when I began putting the date of purchase on my shoes. C'mon … how else will I know when a shoe needs to be retired or if a shoe seems to be wearing better than expected?

Then again, maybe the change was in my socks. No, I don't date the socks. I don't have to. They are numbered sequentially, in pairs. Well, you don't want to put on one sock from a new pair and one from an old pair! They wouldn't feel the same. Plus, some feel better than others for long runs and some are saved for races. Honest!

Or the change could be in my cupboard. There are 159 event T-shirts, an assortment of sweatshirts, running shorts and tights, and one business suit in my wardrobe. And I think I have a tie somewhere.

But not all of the changes were as obvious as these. Some were happening deep inside me, out of my control and without my help.

When I simply ran, I was always relieved to get to the halfway point of a run. I looked eagerly for that spot on the road where I could turn around because it meant I was half-finished. Once I became a runner, I hated to come to that same spot because it meant that I was half-finished with my time of celebration.

When I simply ran, I always held my head down, embarrassed by my speed and my shape. I never made eye contact with anyone I met, and I always turned my head away as cars passed. As a runner, at nearly the same speed and shape, I run with my head held high, greeting everyone and waving at every car. I want to tell each of them, 'Hey, look at me! I'm actually doing this!'

When I simply ran, I was one person against my whole history. As a runner, I am a part of a community of runners. I share in the joy of a victory half a world away and feel the effort of those around me.

It isn't the shoes, socks, clothes or even the speed that makes me a runner. It's running. I pay my membership dues every time I lace up my running shoes. I realize that every time I challenge myself to do more, struggle to get just a little faster, or face the limits of my abilities, I am a runner. A real runner, not just someone who runs.

Waddle on, friends.

Running Home

November 1997

There are many advantages to becoming a runner later in life. There are disadvantages as well – among them, older muscles, older joints and a somewhat more mature physique. Among the advantages, though, is the ability to use running as a means of rediscovering memories long forgotten. Running can be the key that unlocks the most forbidding doors in the cellar of the psyche.

Having had a nonrunning life means that there are people and places that existed for the nonrunning me. As the nonrunner moves further and further into my past, I have found that I need a guide to take me from the person I was to the person I am becoming.

The need for that guide became clear on a recent run through the streets I grew up in. In the suburbs, the edges of the world were defined by your house on one end and the primary school on the other. My world was the roads and alleys and playground that covered an area of just a few streets.

As I ran through my old stomping ground, I was struck first by how small the houses seemed. These monuments to the strength of juvenile male bonding and to the uncertainties of pre-adolescent male-female bonding looked positively ordinary. With just a few strides I was able to run past the houses of old friends and first kisses. Those adult strides helped me understand both the power and the silliness of my memories.

Running further, to the primary school playground, brought me face-to-face with eight years of victories and defeats. From marbles to basketball and baseball, the images were still painfully clear. It was on this nondescript asphalt that I learned what it felt like to punch and be punched, to be in and out of love, to break youthful hearts and to have my own heart and spirit broken. That playground was the site of epic battles for turf, for status and sometimes for nothing at all. As I stood looking at the rusty basketball hoops I wondered what any of it had meant.

I found myself running faster as I strode past the houses of childhood friends who taught me about loyalty and bullies who taught me about pride. I found myself running again with Tommie, Rich and Lester. For the first time in my life, I was running in front. For the first time in my life, I wasn't last.

That day I could have run forever. But just as when I was a child, the time came for me to run home. I had reached the edges of my neighbourhood, the edges of my memories, the edges of my dreams.

What I learned on my run that day was that there are still playgrounds and playing fields and friends and bullies in my life. The battles that I fought as a child are being refought every day in my adult world. I am still seeking to prove to myself and others that I can play their game, that I should be on their team and that I shouldn't be picked last.

And I hope I've learned that the daily victories and defeats in my adult world are only as important as I make them out to be.

Waddle on, friends.

Body of Evidence

March 1998

After exhaustive research, I have finally reached the conclusion that runners' bodies come in three distinct shapes: 1. better than mine, 2. *much* better than mine, or 3. better than mine will ever be.

Where the basic running shape is constructed vertically, my shape is constructed horizontally. Where the best runner's shape goes up, mine goes out. Where a runner's body is long, mine is wide.

Other runners' arms and legs seem to be connected to their bodies at just the right places. Every joint is right where it should be. Every component is in perfect proportion. Their bodies are designed to propel them forwards. Every body part has the single purpose of making running efficient.

By contrast, my arms and legs are connected as if they were an afterthought. Worse, my body looks like it was assembled out of spare parts. I have the legs of a person 1.5 m (5 ft) tall and the torso of someone about 1.9 m (6ft 4 in). Not one component on my body seems to be designed for forward motion. That may explain why I was stationary for 40 years.

When I first started running, I though it was just a matter of time until my shape, which had become well-suited for extended periods of motionlessness, would become a runner's shape. I was sure that my legs would get longer and my torso more aerodynamic.

Somehow I believed that if I acted like a runner and ate like a runner and trained like a runner, eventually I would *look* like a runner.

Not that I really knew what a runner looked like. But I was sure that I would know the running me when I saw him.

I kept watching for the first signs of the metamorphosis – from lumpy to lithe. I knew that my weight was going down. I could measure that. And it did seem to me that there was a little less belly than before. But the basic shape remained unchanged.

The dramatic alignment shift of my body parts didn't happen. My legs looked a little stronger, but they still looked like my legs. And the rest of my body still looked more suitable for sitting than for running.

My investigation into the disparity between runners' bodies and mine was made clear when I shopped for running attire. I guess when you have a runner's shape, the current styles in running clothes make sense. But I'm just not ready to wear a pair of shorts that are cut high enough to expose parts of me normally seen only by my doctor!

Through my research, I also learned that shape isn't always a good predictor of speed. Neither, it turns out, is weight. There have been many occasions when I've been beaten badly by a person whose shape was decidedly round. Wiggle is often superior to waddle.

It's clear to me now that I'll never have a runner's body, no matter how many miles I run. Instead, I'm concentrating on having a runner's soul. I'm doing my best to worry less about the packaging and more about the product.

Maybe then I'll be able to accept that I am more runner than I ever thought I'd be.

Waddle on, friends.

Workin' the Shovel

March 2000

Some of life's lessons I've had to learn only once. For example, don't put your tongue on a frozen flagpole, no matter how funny your friends think it is. Some of life's lessons took me a little longer: don't wait to start a 16-week project until the day before it's due. And I've come to understand that some of life's lessons are, in fact, absolutes. Such as 'thin' is the only word to use in a sentence that contains the word 'hips'.

One of the most important lessons in my life occurred in the blink of an eye. The teacher was someone I barely knew, and the lesson came when I least expected it.

When I was 20 years old, I worked for six months as a labourer on the railways. Our job was to replace broken rails and worn-out ties. Most important, we had to *look* busy. In the yard, this wasn't difficult because there was almost always something to do. But on this day, our only task was to move a large pile of stones from where it was to where the foreman wanted it.

Shovel by shovel, we began carrying rock for the big pile over to a small pile about 30 m (100 ft) down the track. The first shovel didn't seem so bad, but by the tenth one, every muscle started to hurt. With the foreman yelling, I worked as fast as I could and was exhausted in no time. Then, just when I desperately needed some guidance, a teacher appeared.

He was one of the older men on the crew, and he'd been watching me closely. He came over, put his hand on my shoulder and said, 'Son, ain't no man gonna break your back, long as you workin' the shovel.

Let that old man yell. You just work at your own pace.' I looked at him and knew immediately what he meant. It wasn't the foreman who was wearing me out; it was my desire to please him.

I was the one who controlled my effort. I was the one who controlled my fatigue. In the grandest sense, I was the one who controlled my life. It was *my* choice. That day, and every day, I could either work according to my own limits or I could try to live up to someone else's expectations.

My life as a runner began in a similar way to my life as a labourer. I looked outside of myself for guidance. I tried to meet goals that others set for me. I was overwhelmed with 'shoulds'. And I was overcome with failure.

It wasn't until I began to 'work my own shovel' as a runner that running became a constant source of joy instead of a chronic source of frustration. It wasn't until I began to understand that my running really only mattered to me that I was free to run for myself.

Not that running was easy. Like moving stone that day, it's hard to ignore the stares and comments from those who believe I should live up to their expectations. It's hard to run a race with joy when all but one of the water tables have been taken away. It's hard to revel in the mystery of motion when you finish a race alone, the refreshments gone and the clock sitting on a folding chair.

Still I *have* run with joy. And I do.

And when I do – when I overcome my need to please people I don't even know – I hear the voice of my teacher. And I remind myself that my running – indeed, my life – is my shovel. There ain't no man gonna break my back, ain't no man gonna steal my joy, ain't no man gonna rob me of my right to celebrate what I've accomplished, long as I'm workin' the shovel.

Waddle on, friends.

Index

Note: <u>Underlined</u> page references indicate boxed text.

lack of flexibility, 95
muscle imbalances, 95
old shoes, 94, 95
overtraining, 62–63, 69–70,
    72, 73, 93–94
running too fast, 94
running when tired, 94
tripping and falling, 93
twisted ankles, 93
early warning signs of
aches, 69, 89
inflammation, 69
pain, 69, 86, 89–90
soreness, 69, 88–89, 89
stiffness, 69
Injury prevention, 95
recognizing warning signs, 89,
    94
recovery and rest, 38–39, 39,
    95–96
strengthening muscles, 95,
    104
switching shoes, 43, 95
walk breaks, 35
Injury treatment
corrective exercises for, 63
for Illotibial Band Syndrome,
    97–99
orthotics for, 63
patience and discipline during,
    108
for plantar fasciitis, 99–101
RICE therapy for, 96–97
for runner's knee, 103–4
for shinsplints, 104–5
for stress fractures, 102–3
Inner voices. See Criticism, self
Inspiration
burnout from, 16
failed, 16, 113, 118
pep talk for, 118
Intensity of workouts, 69
duration of, 71
frequency of, 70

Interval running, 204
IT Band Syndrome, 97–99

J

Jackets, running, 52
Joints
aches in, 89
injuries in, 88
muscle support for, 88
overuse of, 69
strengthening, 68–69
Joy
in act of running, 167, 169, 171,
    172–73, 219, 227
in being a runner, 170–71
importance of, 178
in one's efforts, 174
in planning runs, 170

K

Kayaking, 159–60
Keeping score
among runners, 175–76
cultural pressure to, 175
giving up on, 177, 178–79, 180
psychic dangers of, 177
temptation to, 174–75
Keeping track of progress,
    177–180
Khannouchi, Khalid, 64–65, 194
Knees
bicycling and, 153
cracking in, 103
pain and swelling in, 98, 103
runner's knee, 103–4
trail running and, 142, 144

L

Left brain, 37–39, 39
Leg lifts, 95
Low arches, 43, 45

236 index

OTHER RODALE BOOKS
AVAILABLE FROM PAN MACMILLAN

1-4050-3338-X	The *Runner's World* Complete Book of Running	*Amby Burfoot*	£18.99
1-4050-4145-5	Marathon Running for Mortals	*John Bingham*	£9.99
1-4050-0665-X	Get a Real Food Life	*Janine Whiteson*	£12.99
1-4050-0673-0	*Men's Health* Home Workout Bible	*Lou Schuler and Michael Mejia*	£15.99
1-4050-2102-0	Lance Armstrong Performance Programme	*Lance Armstrong and Chris Carmichael*	£10.99
1-4050-6717-9	The South Beach Diet Cookbook	*Dr Arthur Agatston*	£20
1-4050-6725-X	The Knee Care Handbook	*Dr Brian Halpern*	£12.99

All Pan Macmillan titles can be ordered from our website, *www.panmacmillan.com*, or from your local bookshop and are also available by post from:

Bookpost, PO Box 29, Douglas, Isle of Man IM99 1BQ

Tel: 01624 836000; fax: 01624 670923; e-mail: *bookshop@enterprise.net*; or visit: *www.bookpost.co.uk*. Credit cards accepted. Free postage and packing in the United Kingdom

Prices shown above were correct at time of going to press.

Pan Macmillan reserve the right to show new retail prices on covers which may differ from those previously advertised in the text or elsewhere.

For information about buying Rodale titles in Australia, contact Pan Macmillan Australia. Tel: 1300 135 113; fax: 1300 135 103; e-mail: *customer.service@macmillan.com.au; or visit: www.panmacmillan.com.au*

For information about buying Rodale titles in New Zealand, contact Macmillan Publishers New Zealand Limited. Tel: (09) 414 0356; fax: (09) 414 0352; e-mail: *lyn@macmillan.co.nz*; or visit: *www.macmillan.co.nz*

For information about buying Rodale titles in South Africa, contact Pan Macmillan South Africa. Tel: (011) 325 5220; fax: (011) 325 5225; e-mail: *roshni@panmacmillan.co.za*